I'm Not the

Girl

I Used To Be

I'm Not the

Girl

I Used To Be

MaHogany Jackson

Lita P. Wood
Editorial Midwife Publishing

Printed in the United States of America
Cover Photo Design: Fostered
www.jus10foster.com

Editor: Lita P. Ward, The Editorial Midwife of LPW Editing & Consulting Services, LLC
www.litapward.com

Dedication

I would like to dedicate *I'M NOT THE GIRL I USED TO BE* to broken women. You are not defined by your mistakes and hardships. Let this book be symbolic that there is light at the end of the tunnel.

Acknowledgements

I would first like to thank God; He is my everything and I am all that I am because of Him. I am thankful for His grace and mercy that has always followed me throughout my journey. As I reflect over my life, over every heartbreak, disappointment, obstacle and situation, He was always there allowing certain situations to happen to steer me in a better direction. Thank You, Lord.

I would also like to acknowledge my husband, Pastor Justin Jackson for never giving up on me or leaving my side throughout my journey. You believed in me before I even believed in myself. You were my first supporter and still to this day, my biggest encourager. I have learned so much about life from you. I honor your leadership because you truly lead by example.

To my twin boys, Justin Marcel Jackson, Jr. and Marcel Mateo Jackson, I love you with every ounce of my being. You challenge me to dream bigger and to settle for nothing less than God's best for my life. In turn, it is my mission to not only teach you that with God anything is possible, but to daily serve as an illustration of His endless possibilities.

To my aunt, Janet Barbour Anderson. I am ever grateful for the meritorious role you played in my life. Thank you for your love, words of wisdom, encouragement, and the countless moments you spent "just being there" for me. I miss you every day, (December 20, 1950-June 15, 2019).

Lastly, I would like to thank my many friends and family members for the influence you all have had on my life. To my parents, stepfather, siblings, grandparents, aunts and uncles, cousins, nieces and nephews, and in-laws. I love each one of you.

TABLE OF CONTENTS

INTRODUCTION

Who I Used to Be

*I*f asked to paint a meaningful picture dating back to one familiar time in my life, the painting would consist of colorful paint splatters, a dab of pink glitter, some jumbled up inspirational words and quotes cut out of magazines, paint skids, garbage, eraser marks, pen swirls...later traced in a purple sharpie marker. I would paint a picture that would appear up close to be an accumulation of clutter and disorder; however, from afar appeal to others as artistry desired. This painting would be an ambiguous fixture to the eye to some, but to me it would reflect oneself – well, who I used to be. It would date back to a time when I was once like that painting - enticing on the outside yet an accumulation of hurt, heartbreak, and insecurity on the inside. Just like that painting, when people looked at me from afar they saw nothing less than skill and ability, but those who took time to view me from up close had a front row seat to my true insecurities. "Out of sight, out of mind" is an idiom most commonly used to express the mere fact that you soon forget people or things when they are no longer present. At times, I had really wished this saying was true; I wished that if someone was absent in your life, it would be easier to get over their absence.

Unfortunately for me, things were much different. Dealing with my father's absence took longer than I would have ever expected, and when I thought I was over it I found myself filling the void of his absence with negative influences and behaviors. Although, my father would sporadically surprise me with teddy bears and cards from time to time, not having my father present as a daily role model left me feeling empty, and secretly envious when I saw him or heard of him spending quality time with his *other* family. My mother was a workaholic. As long as I can remember, my mother has always worked multiple jobs and she enjoyed working - at least that is what she always told me. My mother always made sure I had everything I needed materialistically, yet I longed for more of her physical presence. At times, none of the materialistic things mattered, all I wanted was her attention. My mother strived so hard to "never be like her mother", but in that I believe she became more like her. Always able to provide everything, except her attention. Growing up, the road was lonely. As a junior high student I found myself repeatedly smoking cigarettes around the house, afraid to death that my mother or step-father would pick up the scent from my clothes or hair. I ended up in fights with people I knew I could not beat, simply because I wanted to prove to others my significance and authority; although that plummeted after those fights resulted in recurring losses. Throughout my life I have always stood out; even though, at times I hated it. I tried so hard to fit in and to be normal, but someway and somehow, I always ended up standing out. I was that girl who when caught smoking was given the guidance of "Your worth is far greater than this." Hearing this phrase and phrases similar became annoying and redundant. Why couldn't I just blend into the crowd? It was attention that I wanted, not correction.

Life Lesson: When you are anointed, it does not matter the volume or mass of the crowd you are trying to hide in —you will always stand out.

As a high school student, my emptiness followed, and my insecurities grew. I went into high school with no idea of who I was. I became desperate for male attention, and by the end of my freshman year, nearly every twelfth-grade guy had a nude or pornographic image of me. I began to misuse my birth control pills, by proudly sleeping with multiple guys. I thought I was popular because I was known. I was wrong, but I did not care. My grades started to drop, and I spent more time plugged into negative influences such as drugs, toxic friends, and alcohol. My lifestyle shifted some when I met the guy who I thought was the love of my life.

He was an athlete and tailored to what I thought was my type: tall, dark, and handsome. I fell in love with his allure and charisma, to later find that I was in love with someone who did not love me. I discovered that he was not only charming me, but many others. Still, I did not care. I was addicted to the sex and his fast lifestyle. I was okay with being his "side-chick" because the affection he showed me was more than any I had ever felt. I found myself in constant and continuous drama when it came to dealing with his "main chick" and the others. After a while I grew tired of being in second place and I began to confide into a guy friend of mine. He was frequently known as the "Go-to-Person" for relationship advice. I told him how the guy in my past relationship treated me, and I shared with him how I wanted to be treated. He at the time was in a relationship, and knew almost exactly what I desired. He comforted me in telling me that I deserved everything that I anticipated. I became comfortable and trusted my guy friend in nearly everything he said. It was then when he began to act strange and his dialogue changed. Our conversations would lead to flirting, and our laughs and slaps on each other's backs would lead to intimate, sensual touches. Before I knew it, I was back to square one – second place. He had taken note of the different characteristics that I longed for in a guy and lured me in with those very same tactics that I had described. The only difference from before was that I knew this time that this relationship was not love but lust. After being in and out of his bed, I realized that I wanted different, and this time I meant it. While trying to find my identity, I began to take on the identities of others. I wished to know what it was that drew certain men to their "main chicks", so I begin to act like those girls in particular. I was tired of coming in second place, and I assumed that doing what it was that they did would help me gain first. Unluckily for me, keeping up with everyone else became costly and harder than I expected. I now felt completely out of options. I begin to wonder "why me?" Why couldn't things just work out for me – at least once? It seemed as if my world had just got flipped upside down. My friends turned their backs on me, and before I knew it I was left all alone. I felt so lost, isolated, and purposeless. All the people that I thought I could trust and lean on left and I was left alone to deal with me. I had no idea that this season of isolation would initiate the burial of the "old girl" I used to be and would begin the birthing of the woman I was destined by God to be.

Chapter One
Empty

I was born into a family of hard working women. Many of the women in my family are single, independent mothers with a self-governing mentality. Growing up, my mother included, was a single mother since my father was absent. As a child, my father's absence did not yet affect me in a sense that many of my cousins were raised by single parents as well. As a little girl, I was a deep thinker and dreamer. One evening after returning home after a long day, I asked my mother, "Is this all to life?" She peered at me through the rearview mirror and questioned what I had asked. I went on to explain to her how I felt bored with life. I longed to know whether it was more to life than repeating the same mundane system every day. I was not satisfied with just going to school or going to work and coming back home and starting the cycle back over the next day. I found no joy in that.

My mother answered me by saying, "Yes, you just have to learn how to make the best out of it." At that time, I accepted that answer; however, as I aged I began to understand *that your parents can only expose you to the level in which they have been exposed.* Therefore, what seemed normal to my mother, was normal to her because growing up that was all she was exposed to. My mother later got married and our family began to expand when she had my little sister. It was not until then that I realized that something was not right. I watched how my mother and step-father nurtured my little sister *together* and I began to question my mother about my father. She explained to me how her and my father had separated once I was born. The more she explained, the less I understood. I did not understand how my sister was able to be embraced by both of her parents; meanwhile, I only had one parent to cherish. I started to feel like an outcast, and I began to isolate myself from my mother, sister, and step-father. I felt as if I was intruding on what I thought was the perfect family my sister had between our mom and her father. On family movie nights, I would opt to stay in my room alone instead of joining everyone. My mother noticed the change in my demeanor and reached out to my father. Soon, my father and I began to have phone conversations with each other. I enjoyed every minute of them. I began to feel as if I had a *real* family too.

During this time, I was in elementary school. I was an accelerated student, and I had very close-knit bonds with many of my teachers. I loved to read, and I would constantly receive awards for my academic achievements. One day while at school, I watched how many of the other students had their parents come visit them during lunch. Intrigued by this, I began to ask my father to join me at lunch. He shared with me how he would love to come, and we began to pick dates that worked with his schedule. As the various dates rolled by, he never showed. Shortly after, our phone calls ceased. Heartbroken, it was then that my imagination of having a *real* family shattered. It was not until a couple of years later that my father entered my life again. This time, things were different. I was no longer speaking with my father over the phone, but now in person. I would spend time with my father just about every weekend. The first few months of this, went great. Soon after, my father and his wife began to experience marital issues again. Not to mention, my father and his wife had been married long before I was born. In response to their marital issues, the atmosphere in his home became very tense. My stepmother who at first showed compassion for me began to make indirect statements about me while in my presence. She would say statements about how at times she could not stand to look at me because in me she saw my mother. Her words hurt; however, through this experience, I learned a lot.

Life Lesson: Sometimes you will be prosecuted for things that are beyond your control.

Shortly after, the amount of time that I spent with my father on the weekends began to dwindle. Before I knew it, we were back to not seeing each other at all, despite the various attempts in which I tried to reach out to him to rekindle our relationship. After a while, I grew tired of calling and begging for his time. Hurt, I clung to my mother for attention. As always, my mother worked multiple jobs and her time was limited due to her work schedule. She instead attempted to cheer me up with materialistic things. My mother always talked about how she never wanted to be the type of mother her mother was to her, and she made it her duty to not be. She made sure I was nicely groomed with the latest clothes, shoes, and hairstyles; the things her mother could never provide for her. At times, none of the materialistic things mattered, all I wanted was her attention. My mother strived so hard to "never be like her mother", but in that I believe she became more like her. Always able to provide everything - but her attention. As I graduated to junior high school, I became jealous of many of my friends who lived with both of their parents. I thought that they were lucky to be able to wake up each morning to both of their parents. I saw how their parents spent time with them, and when I compared their life to mine I was always left disappointed. I saw them as a family, yet I did not see the issues and the problems that they faced behind closed doors.

Life Lesson: Too often we compare our lives to others based off what we see. Do not get worked up by someone else's false advertisement.

Junior high school was a constant whirlwind for me. I began with shaky confidence and ended up completely lost and insecure of who I thought I was. In a school full of various types of people, my main goal was to simply fit in. I was tired of feeling like an outcast and I self-assured myself that junior high school would be the place where I would discover others who were similar to me. I was very bright and intelligent; however, it seemed as if my intelligence was what separated me from others. Nearly, every day of my first year in middle school, I was bullied for being different.

Life Lesson: Oftentimes people attempt to label what they do not understand.

In an effort to fit in, I began to focus less on my academics. Since it was my keen abilities that seemed to push others away, I decided to do whatever it took to fit in. It was towards the middle of my seventh-grade year that I began to change my style. My mother never allowed me to wear tight clothing. My jeans would have to be loose, and my shirts could never be too tight on my chest. I hated the way she made me dress, and I was always ridiculed by other girls about my attire. It was then that I started taking matters into my own hands. I started to sneak and pack additional clothes from home that I knew my mother would never allow me to wear to school or even out in public. I would tell my mother to drop me off early at school so that I could eat breakfast at school, yet once I got to school my intentions were very different. I would rush to the girls' bathroom before anyone could see me, and change out of what I wore to school and into the clothes I had secretly packed the night before. Things changed once I began to dress like the other girls. Guys started to pay me more attention, and even the popular girls would invite me to sit with them at lunch. Before I knew it, I was not just sitting with them at lunch but walking with them through the hallways and even sitting with them in class. Hanging with those girls made me feel important and as if I had a voice and opinion that mattered. A lot of things changed once I started hanging with them, not only my style but the way I talked. I began to curse and raise my voice at teachers. My voice and opinion mattered now, so I could say what I wanted, to whom I wanted, when I wanted. At least that is what I thought. Soon, I became just like those girls, yet becoming one was not so easy. My mother did not approve of me wearing makeup. She believed it was too "grown" for girls in middle school to wear makeup, so when we went shopping I would not even ask to go look at the make-up showcase. The only issue was that the girls I hung with wore make-up, and they said if I wanted to look good, I had to get some.

There was no way my mother was going to buy me make-up, so I asked my friends if I could go shopping with them. Once I started going shopping with them, I was able to get my own make-up too, except I was not buying it – I was stealing it. It was okay though, because that is how they got their makeup too. I was scared at first to steal, but after I saw how they did it, I knew I could do it too. Stealing became easy, and when I went out shopping with them we would steal make-up, clothes, and anything else we wanted. It was that simple; if we wanted it, we took it.

Kudos to me.

I wanted to be a part of the popular girl's clique, and finally I was. Hanging out with my new friends was a bliss. I enjoyed every minute of it. Everywhere we went we were the center of attention; from at school in the hallways to on the weekends at the mall. One thing about us is that we loved to party. Nearly every weekend my girls and I would go to a party. Preparing for parties was so much fun. My girls and I would go to the mall the day before the party to gather everything together that we wanted to wear. We would steal any and everything we wanted from the jewelry to the attire and down to the shoes. We had to make sure that we were styled in the latest trends and one of our rules was that we had to wear something new. The day of the party, one of my girls would designate for us to get ready at her house. We would spend hours getting dressed, putting on makeup, and styling our hair and we would never leave the house without taking a few pictures. Once we pulled up to the scene of the party, it was Showtime. Everybody knew us to be one of the highlights of the night. My girls and I would go from guy to guy dancing. One of the reasons guys were so drawn to us at the parties was because of our bodies. We were pretty gifted at our age to have nice hips and thighs and we weren't afraid to show them off. We would grind on the guys and do many of the dances many of the other girls were afraid to try. Partying every weekend was so much fun. It added some flavor to my weekends, and to be honest, I simply enjoyed being a part of the crowd. Once the weekend was over, Monday's at school were the worst. I had not completed any of my homework, so I spent the majority of my mornings copying other students' homework. It was not that I did not know the answers to my assignments,

I just simply had not put aside the time to complete them.

My favorite time of the day was lunch time. Lunch time was when my girls and I would get together to have some real fun. We would laugh and joke about the events of the weekend all lunch period. I had so much fun talking with them, to be honest, I did not care what we talked about. I just cherished the feeling of feeling included. As I continued throughout middle school, my bad habits got worse. During my eighth-grade year, I began smoking Newport cigarettes. Every few days, once school let out, I would walk to the store a few blocks from my middle school and get an older man to purchase one box of Newport "longs" for me. Smoking made me feel powerful and important. It gave me freedom and it filled my void...for the moment. While still in middle school, smoking regularly became a hard habit to maintain. I constantly kept perfume and other fragrances with me to keep the cigarette smell out of my clothes and hair. I knew that if anyone caught me, they would try their best to make me stop the one thing that gave me temporary peace. And as the saying goes, "Brooks make rivers and rivers flow into seas," and so did my insecurities and negative behaviors. Since they were left undealt with, they grew ever more promiscuous and hungry for attention. Smoking cigarettes turned into smoking weed and my attention-seeking mentality evolved into nearly having sex with almost every guy that said he was "fond" of me.

Chapter Two
Desperate

O nce I entered my freshman year in high school things changed – I gained more freedom, more accessibility to people, more time, and more and more ways to be drawn away by my temptations and immature ways. At the time, high school to me was not about grades or academics but rather about being noticed. Feeling as if I was being noticed by others soothed my low self-esteem. Being noticed made me feel as if I was significant or important. Attention was what I craved and I did everything necessary to receive it. Male attention was what I sought after most. I knew that many of the guys that would crowd at my locker day after day only wanted one thing from me – sex. But feeling the heat of the mass attention felt good and that's all I cared about. I struggled so hard when it came to "dating" in my freshman year; it seemed as if all every guy wanted from me was sex. I went from relationship to relationship searching for someone to make me feel complete. I exposed myself multiple times to various guys whether through nude pictures or pornographic videos in an effort to keep them entertained without having to give them sex. I stretched myself so thin in an effort to please them and maintain the relationship, but one after another, each relationship fell through. It was not my prior intentions to be the girl that went from guy to guy but it seemed as if that is what happened when each relationship went tumbling down one after the other.

Life Lesson: I did not recognize it then, but I later realized that everything I did to please those guys did nothing but feed their lustful desires. They were not genuinely interested in me; they were only interested in what I sexually had to offer. I was searching to try to fill a void that I later learned only the Lord could fill. Often times, we search for things to try to fill that emptiness feeling inside of us and many of us seek for attention – in all the wrong places. Others try to fill it with drugs, alcohol, pornography, work and hobbies, but I can most definitely attest to the fact that nothing can ever fill that void but Jesus. Yes, things may at times feel as if they are satisfying those feelings, but it is only temporary. Your wholeness and completeness will never come from the many things you use to occupy your time, but rather your wholeness comes from developing a relationship with the Lord.

I knew that ultimately entertaining these guys would lead up to me eventually having to **give it up.** I remember losing my virginity at the age of 15, while lying outside on the ground one summer night. I had sex with a guy I barely even knew. He had sent me a text a few hours earlier, asking, "When are we going to chill?" I knew his intentions really were not to just hang out and watch Netflix, but as desperate as I was, I invited him to meet me at a family member's house close by where he was currently located. I knew this in particular family member would not be home for a few hours, and I had a key to their house, so I figured it would be a great place to meet up. Once I got there, I freshened up and waited on his arrival. Once he arrived, I invited him in and we sat on the sofa and began to engage in conversation. Moments later, I had my back to the sofa and he was on top of me. As we started to kiss, my heart began to nearly beat out my chest in anticipation for what was next. I knew it would not end there, with just a few kisses, but I knew he was going to want more. I was so scared and nervous; at one point while kissing, he even asked me if I was okay. I suppose he sensed how uneasy I was. I answered him, saying, "Yes." The truth was, I wanted to stop and express that I did not feel ready just yet, but I feared the embarrassment of backing out of it at that point. I figured if I were to do that, he would go and tell all of his friends about how I punked out and I would in response be the laughing stock of my entire high school once I had returned.

Life Lesson: No one person has the power to ruin your entire reputation.

Once our kissing slowed, he asked me if I wanted to go with him on a walk. Puzzled, I said yes, and we stood up and began to walk towards the door. Once we were outside, I turned and locked the door behind me, and we started to walk. After walking a few blocks, we arrived at a slightly lit and hidden area. He smiled at me and took off his jacket. He spread his jacket out on the ground, and told me to lie down. I lied down on top of his jacket and he got on top of me, and we started kissing again. He asked me if I was a virgin and I told him, "Yes." He smiled and began to undress me. After we had sex, we got dressed and began walking back towards my family member's house. I felt uneasy, but it did not matter now. I had already given it up and it was no turning back or undoing the situation.

Life Lesson: Never settle with falling into a situation that could have been avoided due to your fear of what other people may think or say because those same people will not be there when it comes time to clean up the mess of your mistake.

On the way, back to my family member's house, we ran into a girl waiting for us at the corner of the next block. As we approached her, she began to yell and ask us where we had been and what we had done. The guy I was with calmed her down by saying that I was a friend and that we had just went for a walk. She angrily looked at me and began to tell me how she was his girlfriend and that I needed to stay away from her man. Clueless to the fact that he was in a relationship, I started to feel as if I was shattering into a million pieces. My heart sunk and I questioned myself as to how I could have been so naive. The girl walked off and the guy and I continued to walk back to my family member's house. He tried to comfort me in telling me that the girl we had encountered was crazy and that I should not pay her any attention, but I knew that everything he was saying was a lie. He dropped me off at the door and we went our separate ways. Once I got back inside the house, I sat down and began to feel worthless. I felt as if I had made the worst decision of my life and all I wanted to do from then on was bury the memories of what just happened. The next day, the same guy texted me saying how he missed me so much and how he could not stop thinking about me. I ignored every text he sent me and continued with my attempt to forget about what had happened. He continued to reach out to me various times over the following days and weeks, but I knew that I was done with him for good.

A few weeks later, one of my male cousins moved in with my family and I. My family was always the type of people who tried their hardest to help others. My cousin and I already had a close bond prior to him moving in. We and a host of our other cousins would regularly hang out with each other, so by him moving in, it seemed as if I would have the ultimate unlimited hangout partner. Over the next few weeks, we continued to grow closer and get to know each other even the more. I shared with him my experience of losing my virginity and he gave me advice from the male perspective on what I should have done in that situation. From then on, I began to confide in my cousin about nearly every guy I was interested in dating. I would seek advice from him as to what I should do in various relationship situations. About a month or two later, things began to change within my cousin's and I relationship. He would make certain flirtatious gestures and remarks towards me and I would entertain his behavior by dressing more promiscuous when alone with him and engaging in lecherous conversations. We both knew that what we were doing was wrong, but we continued anyway. One late night while laying on my bed, I saw someone peer into my bedroom through the crack in my door. Once I realized it was my cousin, I invited him in to sit on the edge of my bed to watch television together. After a few minutes went by, he turned around and looked at me. He then slowly lifted the blanket sheets at the edge of my bed and started to move towards me while under the sheets. Hesitant at first, I gave in to my lustful desires and had sex with my cousin. From that point on, we had sex various times and we even started to secretly date. Our "relationship" went on for multiple months until my mother found out and forced him to move out. By then, we had engaged in sexual intercourse more times than I could even count. Once he moved out, and we began to see each other less often, our communication started to dwindle. We soon after went our separate ways.

Life Lesson: Do not give in to temptation. "Temptation comes from our own desires, which entice us and drag us away. These desires give birth to sinful actions. And when sin is allowed to grow, it gives birth to death" (James 1:14-15 (NLT))

After my cousin and I went our separate ways, feelings of self-guilt and insecurity began to overtake me. As the weeks went by, I would regularly catch my mind wondering off and reflecting on the series of events that led up to my cousin and I sleeping together. I dreaded the thought of how I allowed such behavior to go on for so long. I looked at myself as worthless and desperate to have even thought that my cousin and I would even be able to have a relationship. To quickly swallow up the very thoughts and feelings concerning my cousin and me, I began to stroll through the back of my mind and cell phone contact list searching for someone to fill the worthlessness I felt inside. It was not that I liked the idea of jumping from one guy to the next, but having someone else to focus my attention on seemed to simmer the pain of the previous mess I had created.

While in the midst of this, my freshman grades academically were horrible. With all the chaos going on in my life (*that I had created*), I had little time for focusing on school or my grades. For the first time, I had received my first F on an assignment. Many of my teachers questioned me about my poor performance in class and I would reply saying that I had ongoing family issues that distracted my focus from class and schoolwork. Although that was a lie, I did not feel the need to share with them the truth. It was not that I could not focus, but instead that I *chose* not to. The curriculum and assignments were not academically challenging to me at all, but rather I decided to focus more on the things that I thought were important such as friends, relationships, parties, weed and alcohol. One thing that did not end when my cousin and I went our separate ways was my craving to smoke weed. Smoking seemed to hide the pain of everything that I was facing in my life. Weed clouded my thoughts concerning my poor grades. Weed gave me the false hope and impression that despite all the mess I was creating in my life, things were still going to be alright. Weed made me feel important and powerful. It allowed me to take a temporary trip away from my problems and issues. Weed and alcohol were my pick-me-uppers when I wanted to hide from the pain. Besides, having friends and family members that smoked and drank alcohol gave me more accessibility to it and the ability to have others to share my temporary vacations with. Over the next few months, every new relationship I entered following the forbidden fling with my cousin were all very short and temporary. They barely lasted over a month. At this point, I was not interested in a long-term relationship, but rather someone I could have fun with and talk dirty to; someone that was okay with being just friends with benefits. I was not proud of the idea of being a call girl, but the sensuous attention aroused me. I knew that the various guys I dealt with did not truly care about me, but living in the heat of the moments when it felt like they did satisfied me. *One thing for sure, it did not take long for me to become well known within my school.*

Chapter Three
What I Thought Was Love

*O*ne day a guy messaged me on Facebook. *(Facebook is a popular free social networking site that makes it easy to connect and share with your friends and family online.)* It was not anything out of the ordinary for guys to message or inbox me on social media; it was rather common that instances like this would take place. My social media inboxes stayed filled with flirtatious comments from guys, and many of them would send me various messages to see if I wanted to hang out and "chill" with them. I was always very selective of the messages that I chose to respond to on social media. Many of the guys that messaged me on social media had never seen me a day in their life. A couple of them were single, some of them were in relationships, and others were even married. They all would message me based off their liking of my half nude photo postings on social media, in hopes that I would respond back to them and entice their desperate desires. Unfortunately, in their case, I would rarely ever respond. I was more interested in guys that I knew and were willing to express their interest in me in person. Therefore, when this one guy named Terrence messaged me, I did not respond right away. Instead, I clicked on his profile and began scrolling through his recent postings and pictures. After viewing a few of his pictures, I began to recognize him from a few of the parties I had attended in the past.

Since we lived in a small town, there were only two high schools. And just like any other place, those schools were rivals. Well, it just so happened that he attended our rival high school, which made it even more exciting. With all this in mind, and the fact that he was quite fine, I decided that I would message him back. After chatting with him for a few minutes over Facebook, I decided to give him my number, so we could continue our conversation over text messages. As we continued the conversation over text, he began to share with me how he had decided to message me because of how attractive I was, and how he was interested in getting to know me on a more personal level. The more we talked, the more he lured me in with every word of his enticing charisma. The next day, I shared with my close friends how Terrence had reached out to me. After showing them his pictures, they in agreement admitted that he was extremely good looking, and they all encouraged me to continue getting to know him. I had also texted one of my close male cousins sharing with him the news about Terrence. His response, on the other hand was very different from everyone else's. He encouraged me to do the very opposite of what my friends had said. He began telling me that Terrence was a player, he had many girlfriends, and that he was not worth my time. Not wanting to hear his advice, I completely disregarded his advice and did not respond back to his message. I had already made up in my mind that I was going to give this guy a chance and I was not going to allow anyone to change my mind – even family.

Life Lesson: God always sends us a warning, whether it be through a person, a sign, or a dream. Pay attention.

The more Terrence and I talked, whether through text messages or phone calls, the more I became interested in him. Over the next week or so, we grew to know each other more and we began to grow closer. We would meet up with each other at parties and sporting events and would mingle together. I loved every moment I spent with him. I began to treasure our relationship, in hopes that we would have a future together. He was everything that I thought, at the time, I wanted in a man. He was an athlete and had a smile that would light up any room he entered. He had a great sense of humor and fitted like a glove within my "must-be" desired physical description for a man which was tall, slim, dark, and handsome. After about two and a half weeks of getting to know Terrence, he invited me for the first time, to come over to his house. Since we would typically get together at sporting events and dance parties, this was going to be the first time we would be able to be in an environment alone. When we first got to his house, his mother was sitting downstairs in the living room watching television. We greeted her and then he led me straight upstairs. He did not even introduce me to his mother. Once we got to the top of the stairs, he directed me to turn right and then we walked into his room. Once we got into his room, he began to clean off his bed by removing an ashtray and a few other possessions that were laying spread out on his bed. Once he was finished, we sat down on his bed, and he turned on the television. He scrolled through the channels until he found the sports channel. On the television screen, it displayed the ending of a Miami Heat vs Boston Celtics basketball game. We started watching the game and engaging in conversation. We talked for a while about basketball, who were the best basketball players, teams and so on. I honestly was not familiar with the game of basketball, but to keep the conversation going, I threw out a few basketball names and teams I knew and we debated until I finally told him that he was right. Once the basketball game ended, he stretched back on his bed and I turned around to face him. He began looking at me with his suave brown eyes and charming smile. He signaled his hand in a direction for me to come closer. I laid beside him and we looked into each other's eyes. He smiled and began to kiss me. We kissed and kissed until he was finally on top of me. Once on top of me, he looked into my eyes and began to tell me how sexy I was. I blushed and began to stare into his big brown eyes. We both knew what was next. He took off his shirt and began to undress me. Once undressed – we had sex.

Life Lesson: When you are dating someone or in a relationship, go on dates! A date is not going to his house and laying on the couch watching Netflix. A date is taking a walk together, going out to eat or to the movies. Do activities that allow you both to really get to know each other. Furthermore, when I say get to know each other, I mean more than their last name, favorite color, or favorite sports team. Find out what they like and do not like, what makes them happy or sad. Ask them questions like what are their goals, where do they see themselves in 10 years, and so on. Begin to build the foundation of your relationship with stability grounded in friendship. The problem with many of us is when we first begin dating or pursuing a relationship, one of the first things we do is have sex. When you have sex so early within a relationship, your mind and perspective from then on is misconstrued and a soul tie is formed. From then on, things you would have not allowed or thought were acceptable before, you will now allow from that individual because you are emotionally blinded. That is why it is so hard to get out of a relationship that you know is not good for you, when sex has been involved.

After I left Terrence's house that day, we texted my entire drive home. Once I got home and were settled, I called him and we talked over the phone for the next few hours until he told me he had somewhere to go and would talk to me later. Moments felt like hours, when I was not texting or talking to him over the phone. I stayed up waiting for him to call me back that night, but he never called. Finally, he texted me "good night" with a heart symbol attached. I texted him back replying "good night babe" with the same heart symbol attached. Once I sent him the text, I began to stare at the ceiling with the biggest smile on my face. My night had been made. The next morning when I woke up, I began to reflect on the events that had happened on yesterday. I knew deep down that having sex with Terrence so soon was probably not the best decision I could have made - but I did not care. For the very first time, I felt loved. As weeks went on, our relationship grew deeper. Terrence and I began to spend more and more time together. Whether I went over his house, or got together with him at a friend's home, we were always and in some way together, and I was happy. It was as if I finally felt content and had some type of peace with how things were going in my life. Were things perfect between us? No, but for once in my life, I did not feel ashamed or insecure about my current relationship. It was as if he made me feel secure by filling my emptiness. When I was with him, I felt like a million bucks. When I was with him, he made me forget about all my worries. When I was with him, I felt empowered. The affection he showed me was like none I had ever received before. Spending time with him made me forget about all the other guys of my past. All I wanted was him and at the time it seemed like all he wanted was me.

One thing for sure, every time Terrence and I got together we had sex. The sex was amazing and every time we had sex, it felt like it drew us even closer. Terrence was an exotic guy and every time we had sex, we tried something new. Whether it was trying a different position or simply changing and spicing up the location. He without a doubt pleased me and made me feel good. Things between Terrence and I continued to go smooth. We would see each other weekly and talk to each other daily. About three months into our relationship, my feelings for him began to grow more intimate. For the very first time, I began to feel more than just loved but in love. Every time I would hear his voice or his ringtone on my phone, my heart would skip a beat. Each time I heard his voice, it would remind me of the way he would grab me in his arms, and whenever I was in his arms, I longed to stay there forever. Being in his arms made me feel secure and fulfilled. When I was not with him, I felt lonely. It was as if I lived for his phone calls and craved the time we spent together. Without it, I felt bare and useless. It was as I had begun to form my identity in him. With him by my side, I knew who MaHogany was. MaHogany was a girl that was loved and was loved by him. As the weeks continued to go by, Terrence and I began to proudly display our relationship while in the presence of others. The more we would conceitedly show affection towards one another in the presence of others, the more the gossip began to stir up. I suddenly started to receive numerous questions concerning the status of our current relationship. People wanted to know how long we had been together, when we got together, and so on. I eagerly shared with them the details concerning my new relationship. *I mean, there wasn't anything to hide, right?* Soon after sharing those details, rumors, at least that is what I thought they were at the time, began to spread about my new relationship. People were saying that he was "playing" me and that he had other girls on the side. At first, I did not pay the gossip and drama any attention, I instead suggested to myself that all the commotion was most likely coming from a few envious individuals with nothing better to do with their time but spread lies and create drama concerning my new relationship. I was stopped in my tracks though, when I began to receive text messages and phone calls from his "other girls." Completely in disbelief, I immediately called Terrence and questioned him about the girls that had contacted me. He comforted me in saying that he did not talk to those girls anymore, and that he used to talk to them in the past. After talking to him over the phone, I felt better about the entire situation. I concluded that those girls were probably jealous girls of his past who were simply trying to get me worked up for no true reason at all.

The next day, while at school I began to share with a few of my close girlfriends what had happened on the past night. Many of them looked at me confused, puzzled by the fact that I believed what Terrence had told me. I tried to reassure them that I could trust

Terrence and that I could tell from his voice that he was not lying. My closest friend at the time insisted that I not believe his lies and end the relationship before it got worst. I, however, at the time did not want to hear any of the advice my friends were trying to give me. They did not know Terrence like I did nor had they spent the amount of time that I had spent with him. Who were they to judge or dictate my relationship? That night while talking to Terrence over the phone, I insecurely asked him the question "what are we" in terms of the status of our relationship. I simply wanted and desired some clarity and surety in our relationship. This was not the first time I had asked him this question. However, many of the times that I asked him this question he would reply using unclear phrases like "we are just talking" or he would say "you know you my girl." This time though when I asked him this question, I was looking for a different response. We at the time had been together for about five months and I was looking for a more solid answer. I was ready to hear him use the terms that I was his girlfriend and that he was my boyfriend. I was tired of the unclear responses. *I mean we were doing everything boyfriend and girlfriends did, right?* So why couldn't he just give me the title of being his girlfriend? Unfortunately, he responded the same way he always did. Disappointed, I took his answer without further discussion. I guess all I would ever be to him was just "his girl." I tucked my feeling in my pocket and changed the subject. Once I got off the phone with him, I began to feel insecure and worried. Maybe since I was just "his girl" he could be messing with other girls on the side. I did not however let those thoughts wonder in my mind long. I began to refocus my mind on the good times we shared together and as a result my mood and spirit began to lift instantly.

I was determined I was not going to let those girls or even my friends cause me to question my relationship. The constant love Terrence showed me in person and through conversation had not changed, so I was not going to let anyone's opinion of my relationship get to me. As long as I was happy, that was all that mattered. Even if he was messing with those other girls, as long as the affection he showed me did not change, I did not care. They were side chicks anyway, so if they chose to linger on the side, I was not going to let that be my problem.

Life Lesson: If you claim to be in a relationship with an individual and they cannot give you a clear answer concerning the status of the relationship that is a red flag that he or she does not value your relationship enough to give it a clear title. If someone truly values their relationship with you, they will have no issue clearly identifying the status of the relationship. This could also be a sign that the individual you are in a relationship with does not see a future with you. Phrases like "it is complicated" are not acceptable responses or is accepting the excuse that someone has trust issues or is scared to label the relationship because they fear commitment or titles. If that is the case, they should not be seeking to be in a relationship. Also, cheating is never okay within a relationship. If someone truly values you and the assets you bring into their life, they will not cheat on you. Be mindful, cheating does not solely take place when the individual you are in a relationship with sleeps with someone else or even secretly has conversation with someone else. Cheating starts when that individuals sees someone attractive walk by and they take a second look. Signs of cheating appear long before that individual has sex with someone else. Lastly,

there is not a difference between a "main chick" and a
"side-chick." If you are in a relationship with someone,
you and that other individual should be both giving
each other 100% of your time and commitment. If
someone cannot give you 100% of their time and
commitment that could be a sign that you do not need
to be in a relationship with that individual. Even if the
individual you are in a relationship with gives you
80% of their time and gives other girls 20%, that is not
okay nor should you allow that to be acceptable. You
should never have to share your "man" or "woman"
with anyone. If you have to share your significant
other with others that is a sign that you need to end
the relationship.

As time went on, girls continued to contact me about
their dealings with Terrence and it became clear that
he was messing with other girls. Completely
heartbroken and lost on what to do, I accepted his
behavior and continued to move forward with our
relationship. I felt as if I had no one to turn to; at least
no one that would give me the advice I wanted to hear.
I had friends to call, but I knew that they would give me
the same advice they had given me before, which was

to end the relationship and move on. But that was not what I wanted to hear. I wanted someone to tell me that it would be alright and that he would change. I loved him so much and all I wanted was for things to work and get better. Over the next few months, things between Terrence and I began to slow down. When he would come over, he would not stay long and all it seemed like he wanted was sex. I tried to buy him materialistic things and neglect my priorities in order to give him *even* more of my time, to show him how much I truly cared for him. Unfortunately doing this changed nothing; things only got worse. When I would get on social media, I would see him publicly flirting with other girls through conversation and when I would ask him about it, he would say that his words were not intended to be taken that way. It seemed as if all he was doing was adding to the heap of lies he had already accumulated. At this point, many thoughts ran through my head. Why was this happening? He did not act like this in the beginning, so why did it seem like things were spinning out of control nine months into our relationship? Where did we go wrong? What did I do so wrong?

Life Lesson: Often times when things feel like they are spinning out of control within our relationships, we suspect the cause of the conflict we are facing is due to a recent incident; however, in most cases situations within our relationships become out of control due to the accumulation of us neglecting the smaller issues that rise within our relationship. If you catch your significant other flirting through small talk with other girls and you do not address it, then later you find him privately texting other girls in secret and you do not address it, you cannot claim to be overwhelmed nor surprised when he eventually publicly flirts with other girls while with you or within a public atmosphere. The point I am expressing is that if you do not address the issue and put an end to certain behaviors within your relationship, you will make room for those situations to grow worse.

But despite all the lies, headache, and confusion I was experiencing, it still seemed as if I could not let him go. Even though I knew he was messing around with other girls, it was something that still drew me to him. I was so in love with him and I had invested so much time into him that giving up on this relationship was the last thing I wanted to do. Yes, I was hurt by his actions and the thought of knowing that he would be at my house one minute and with someone else the very next minute tore me to pieces, but I did not want to let go. It was getting to the point where he would even make prideful remarks towards me like: "You'll be right back" or, "We'll see how long this last" when I would tell him I was leaving or done with him due to his actions and behavior. It was as if he used the very platform of knowing I was not going to leave him as a stage to continuously break my heart. We were about 11 months into the relationship when I first started to publicly see him in pictures with other girls at parties or even at their houses. I would question him about the pictures, and I would always get the same response. He would say that the picture was not intended to be taken that way, and that the girl and him were just friends, or he would even try to flip the situation back on me and say that I was always accusing him of cheating and since I thought he was cheating, he claimed I would always take pictures and social media postings out of context. I knew, however, that at this point every answer he came up with was a lie. All his responses did were caused me to get even more frustrated with him and secretly envious of the other girls I saw him go after. Those other girls knew about me, so why were they still entertaining him? The thought of those girls spending more time with him than I did made me furious and I began to despise those other girls. What was wrong with me that made me not enough for him? I began to examine the other girls that he would go after to see what it was about them that caused Terrence to be so attracted to them. As I began to look and study the other girls, I started to feel as if every bit of security and self-esteem I had gained while in this relationship was slowly and painfully being washed down the drain. Who was I? I did not even know how to answer that question on my own. It seemed as if I had spent so much time trying to give and show Terrence how much I loved and cared about him that I had forgotten about myself and my identity as an individual. Maybe what attracted him to these other girls was their unique style and self-confidence. I figured that if I gained style and confidence, I would have the ability to win him back.

During this time, Terrence was in the process of transferring to my high school. I was tremendously excited that he and I would be now attending the same high school. I was now ever more determined and motivated to win him back, over the next few weeks, through my style and self-confidence since I would now have the opportunity to see him every day throughout school. There would be no way he would not want to drop his other girls once he saw the instant change in me. At the time, my wardrobe was fair. I dressed up to date, following the latest trends and fashion; however, I was determined to take it up a notch. I went from wearing casual sneakers and flat shoes to wearing heels with nearly every outfit. I wore less jeans and more dresses, skirts, and short shorts. I would secretly stalk the Facebook and Instagram pages of the other girls' he was attracted to, in order to see what type of clothes they wore and how they wore them. Then I would mimic their styles. If they wore high-waist jeans, I wore high-waist jeans. If they wore a crop top with a long skirt, I would go out to the mall the next day searching for a similar crop top and long skirt. The only difference between their outfits and mine was simply the color. One of the girls noticed how I copied her outfits and would whisper to her friends about me when I would walk pass her at school or at different parties and sporting events; however, I did not care. I was more focused on my main goal which was to *fully* win my man back. The harder I tried to win my man back, the more time went by and things seemed to get worse. I began to feel as if I was officially losing to these other girls. Things really shifted within our relationship when he decided to privately take another girl out on a date to one of the fancier restaurants in our city. At this point I realized that I had officially lost and that now I was no longer anything more to him but a girl on the side. As I reflected over our relationship, I realized that not one time had he taken me on an actual date. Our dates entailed watching television together or me spending the night with him. They were never as nice as actually going out to a restaurant. The night of his date I laid in bed and cried myself to sleep. But as I expected, the next day he reached out to me as if nothing had ever happened, and guess what? I responded back to him as if nothing had even bothered me and as the weeks went on... I kept sleeping with him.

Chapter Four

Addicted

*T*he following weeks after Terrence's date with another girl were very uncomfortable. Terrence knew that I was aware of him going out on this date; however, if I was not going to confront him about it...he was not going to mention it to me. I felt like at this point, confronting him about his date was not going to do anything beneficial, but cause more tension and distance between the two of us. At this point, Terrence knew my limits and my weakness, and since he knew I was too tired and weak to address him about his continuous interactions with other girls, he used me as a constant doormat. The truth was, I was too tired of fighting and always having to confront him about other girls, but I was also too desperate to want to end the relationship and let him go for good. As a result, communication between Terrence and I became dreadfully distant. I would send him a text message, and I would not hear back from him until several hours later. This was very discomforting to me because Terrence always had his phone with him and in his hand. He would post on Facebook, Twitter, and various other social networking outlets several times a day before I would even receive a text back from him. When I would call him on the phone, he would never answer. It was as if our entire communication was restricted to communicating through text messages. The only time I would get a chance to see him was when he would come over my house. Even then, when he would come over, he would not stay long. He would at the most stay over for an hour and within the time we spent together, all he wanted to do was have sex and then out the door he went. It was clear to me now, that I was nothing more to him than an option.

Life Lesson: What you do not uproot in your relationship will continue to grow, and at some point, the mess that you chose not to uproot will begin to uproot you. When the individual that you are in a relationship with realizes that you will tolerate anything, they will treat you any kind of way. Moreover, when we find ourselves in these type of relationships, the first thing we want to do is try to fix it. However, the sad truth is that if you are in a relationship with someone and they are mistreating you because of your high tolerance, chances are the best thing you can do for that relationship is to exit it. When someone truly values you, he or she will be more interested in uplifting and nurturing your growth than looking for ways to manipulate you.

The next three months of our relationship continued to go downhill and get worse. Everything from how Terrence and I interacted with each other to our sex life changed. When Terrence and I would have sex, it was as if he barely wanted to kiss me. It seemed as if all genuine intimacy between us was slipping away. I began to feel like nothing more than a booty call to him. The sad part was that I was so attached to him and in love that every time he called, I would answer. I felt so degraded, but I was so addicted and attached to him. Now, when he would see me in school, he would barely even speak. He made it appear as if we were no longer in a relationship while in the presence of others. However, when he would text me later that day, his dialogue was very different. When we would communicate through text messages, he would make it seem as if I was the crazy one, and that he was not trying to act distant towards me in front of others. I was not that foolish, to not recognize the true distance his constant actions displayed. As the weeks went by, it felt as if I was constantly going in circles. When I would get mad at Terrence, because of his lies and cheating, he would send me dainty flirtatious messages like "I miss you", "I want you back", and so on until I gave in and lost my attitude with him. Once I would lose my attitude, he would want to come over. Once he came over, the drill was always the same. He would sweet talk me and we would have sex. After the sex, he would become distant, and I would see or hear about him cheating again. I would as a result, confront him about it, and I would tell him that I was done with the relationship. A day later, he would send me several flirtatious messages, I would give in, he would come over, and the cycle continued to repeat repetitively. After cycling through the cycle week after week, I began to feel so worthless. I would at times even start to feel depressed. My close girl friends would always encourage me to leave Terrence, but I felt like I was in too deep to leave. Yes, feeling like a revolving door to Terrence hurt, but I did not want to give up on him for good. I felt like if I were to let him go, I would be giving up on the 15 months I had invested into our relationship. I felt like if I was to leave, who would want to be with me? I felt like if I was to leave, I would never be able to love someone as much as I loved him. These reasons alone left me paralyzed. The fear of leaving was so intense that I felt more comfortable enduring the pain and simply staying with Terrence. Going through these cycles with Terrence broke me down so bad mentally and emotionally. The constant hurt and baggage I carried around every day felt unbearable. It was as if my world was centered on Terrence, and without him, I could not function and live.

One day, I was invited by someone to attend a church service at a church within my local community. The service was extremely enlightening and I fell in love with the preaching style of the head pastor of the church. I was amazed by the way the pastor could effectively deliver his message in a way that was comprehensible to everyone. I also loved how transparent he was when explaining certain topics and situations. I knew then that I wanted to attend another one of his church services. Growing up, my family and I were not people that regularly attended church. My family claimed to believe in Jesus and the Bible, but their actions never reflected it. When my family and I would sporadically attend church together, we would attend churches that I felt never effectively addressed the issues I faced daily. I figured that if I wanted to attend another one of this pastor's church services I would most likely have to go alone. I was so eager though to hear another one of this pastor's messages that I did not care if I had to go all by myself. Something in me made me feel as if I was to attend this church; I could possibly learn ways to cope with my current relationship. After attending this church for a few weeks, I grew to love the church more and more. The regular attendees of the church were very friendly. I even had a chance to meet the pastor, who was also extremely warmhearted. One Sunday, after the pastor preached his sermon, I decided to join the church. I felt that this was the next step to take since I enjoyed attending the church so much. I loved how the pastor preached on the issues that I faced on a regular basis within his sermons. He even spoke on issues concerning my relationship, and because he did so, my eyes were opened to a lot. When I first started attending the church, I was not too eager to hear the pastor's sermons on relationships, because they all reflected the fact that I needed to let Terrence go.

However, the more I listened to his sermons, I understood why I needed to let him go, and instead of dreading the pastor's sermons on relationships, I learned to love them. I looked at this church as my way out of the relationship Terrence and I had. Now, when I would experience the same cycle with Terrence, I would start to feel conviction. *(Conviction is when you feel guilty about a sin you committed.)* I would feel convicted because I knew from my pastor's sermons that fornication was a sin, and how that sin can have a negative effect on your life. *(Fornication is when you have sex with someone that you are not married to.)* As I continued to go through the cycles with Terrence, the greater the conviction I felt, and the more I wanted to end the relationship between Terrence and I. I got to the point where after I would have sex with Terrence, I would cry because I felt so convicted. I knew that Terrence was not good for me and it became even more apparent that I needed to end the relationship immediately.

Life Lesson: When trying to overcome certain situations, habits, and obstacles within your life, it is so important to regularly attend a Bible-based church. What I mean by "Bible-based" is a church that *teaches the Word of God in a way that you understand. You may be thinking...Don't all churches teach the Word of God? No! Not all churches teach the Word of God; many churches are more concerned with being liked than helping others overcome their struggles. What I mean by that is that many churches would rather preach what people <u>want</u> to hear versus what they <u>need</u> to hear. Start attending a church that teaches the Bible, and teaches it in a way that you understand. It is not okay to attend just any church. In order to successfully overcome your struggles and situations, you need to attend a church that teaches the Word of God in a way that you can understand and are able to apply the Word to your life. This may require you to have to stop attending the church your entire family grew up in or even the church your parents' pastor. Your soul and understanding of the Word of God is more important than attending a church that does not help you, to simply make others happy. They will understand later on, and if they do not, that is okay too. The church that I attended in that particular season of my life, I no longer attend. I believe that certain churches are for specific seasons.*

One Tuesday night, while entertaining the same cycle with Terrence, he messaged me asking if I wanted to come over to his house after school the next day. The first thing that came to my mind was the fact that I had Bible study Wednesday evening. I immediately felt convicted knowing that I needed to decline Terrence's offer and leave him alone for good. I instead allowed my feelings to get the best of me, and I told him that I would come over directly after school. While in school on Wednesday, I debated and debated whether I was going to go over Terrence's house. When the last bell rung for school to end, I made the decision to ignore what I knew to be right, and instead go to Terrence's house. As I pulled up to Terrence's house, I started to get nervous. I was not nervous about having sex with Terrence, but instead nervous because I knew God would not be pleased with me if I ignored His instruction and had sex with Terrence. I swallowed hard as I got out of my car and I walked up to Terrence's door. I knocked on the door and Terrence opened it. We both knew the drill, we chatted for a while, and then we had sex. After I left Terrence's house I cried all the way to Bible study. I felt so stupid for falling into the same trap again. While attending Bible study, I felt so disappointed in myself that I could not even participate during the worship segment. I was distraught and you could see it on my face. I made up in my mind that from that day forward I was done with Terrence. After Bible study was over, I went searching for a woman named Jessica that attended the same church as I did. Jessica typically stuck around after Bible study was over and mingled with many of the other regular attendees. Jessica was a mentor of a couple of the young adults at our church. I knew that Jessica would be one of the best people to talk to concerning my relationship with Terrence. Once I found Jessica, I gave her my phone number and told her to give me a call once she got home from church. On my way home from church, I thought about how serious I was to be done with Terrence. I was tired of the cycles, and I knew I deserved better. About an hour after I got home, Jessica gave me a call. While on the phone with Jessica, I jumped straight to the chase. She did not know much about me, and I did not know much about her. All I knew was that I felt led to talk to her about this situation. I explained my relationship with Terrence to Jessica, and she instructed me to disconnect from Terrence immediately. She told me the best way to disconnect from him would be to block him from texting and calling my phone and from contacting me on social media. I was hesitant at first about blocking Terrence because I was not sure if I was quite ready to completely disconnect from Terrence. I explained to her how I had just been to Terrence's house that day and that if I just randomly blocked him without sending him an explanation that it would not make sense. She still encouraged me to block him immediately by explaining to me that he did not value me and that technically Terrence and I were not in a relationship, and that I was just a revolving opportunity for sex to Terrence. Her transparency hurt, but it healed me in the end. I listened to her and blocked Terrence from contacting me over the phone and on social media.

Life Lesson: In that season of my life, Jessica was a mentor sent by God to help me. Although I reached out to her for the advice and mentoring, God was still the one who led me to her. Without listening to Jessica's instructions, I would not be where I am now. When you believe that God has assigned a mentor to you, no matter how uncomfortable their advice may be, take it. Your mentor is similar to your doctor in a sense that, he or she may have to cut you (hurt your feelings through transparency) to heal you (help you overcome your situation). I am so glad I listened to Jessica. I do not have regular communication with Jessica now, but in that season, Jessica was one of my biggest supporters and encouragers. Do not ignore and neglect whom God sends or directs you to as a mentor.

How to Disconnect from an Unhealthy Relationship

If you are in a relationship that you know needs to end, here is a proven and successful 5-step process that I have generated to help you disconnect in a healthy manner. I am not at all saying that this process is easy, but if you are extremely determined to end your unhealthy relationship, it will work.

1. **Make up in your mind that you are done.**
   a. This is the first step, and one of the most important steps. If you do not officially make up in your head that you are completely done with your significant other, then this process will be pointless. You will later find yourself

quitting this process and going back to your unhealthy relationship. You must decide in your mind that no matter what he or she says, you are done. It is also helpful to make a list of reasons why you are ready to let go of the unhealthy relationship. This list will give you motivation later on when your heart wants to go back, but your mind knows better.

2. **End all contact**

   a. When I say end all contact, do so entirely. This step involves blocking that individual from calling and contacting you over the phone and on all your social media networking sites. You should also go a step further by doing the same to all his close relatives and friends. It sounds harsh now, but you will appreciate it later. If any of them ask why, it is safe to tell them that you are doing what is best for you when it comes to moving on from the relationship. Ending all contact is so important because you close the loopholes in which your ex could try to use to contact you and lure you back in with his or her same manipulating tactics. It is time for your heart, mind, and spirit to get a rest. Blocking the individual also helps because it aids the "moving on" process; i.e. out of sight, out of mind. No, this does not mean that it will be easy to forget them, but it will be a bit easier trying to move on. It also puts up a safety guard from them to contact you and you trying to contact them. Now, once you block them, do not go back checking to see how they are doing without you. That should no longer be your concern. What they do and whom they do it with should not be your priority. You must move on. Yes, it will hurt, but it is best for you in the end, I promise.

3. **Change your surroundings.**

   a. If you and your ex used to go to certain restaurants and locations together, try your best to avoid those places. You cannot risk being flooded with those thoughts and memories while going through this process. If you and your ex attend the same school, as Terrence and I did, avoid that individual as much as possible while at school. Go a different way within the hallways; try to switch lunches or seats in the classroom. Do whatever you can to protect your peace. Also, if you and your ex have mutual friends, explain to your friends that you do not want to hear about anything concerning your ex. If they are truly your friends, they will respect your request.

4. **Insolation**

   a. During this time of moving on, you are going to most likely find yourself in periods of isolation. If you and your ex spent a lot of time together, not being with that individual will leave you with a lot of time on your hands. Instead of waddling in your sorrow, be proactive with your time. Get involved in things that interest you. Join a small group, volunteer, hang out with family and friends, learn a skill, tackle a new adventure, travel, journal, etc. Take this time to get to know yourself. Many times, we know more about other people than we know about ourselves.

Take this time to explore your interests, and discover your purpose or true calling in life. Learn what makes you happy, sad or indifferent. Discover your style and niche. Learn about you. Trust me; there is so much more than you think to learn about yourself.

5. **Wait on God**

    a. Lastly, wait on God. Be patient and wait on God to send you a godly man or woman. Do not go about trying to pursue different people and relationships in hopes to fill the emptiness your ex left you feeling inside. Instead, trust in the Lord with your love life. He did not fail me, and He will not fail you. There is someone out there for you that will love you for you, and will not hurt you the way your ex did, but you have to wait. Yes, waiting is hard, but it is best. Trust me; it will pay off in the end. I am a living witness that it will.

Chapter Five
Downhill

*E*ach day I went without having contact with Terrence was hard. I would have to constantly fight the urge to want to unblock him and see if he had sent me any text messages or left me any voice mails. I longed to know whether he missed me. When I would see him at school, he would act distant towards me as usual; however, after about a week went by of us having no communication in person or through text message, when we would end up alone in the hallway at school together, he would try and call my name and get my attention. I suppose he was finally beginning to realize that his messages and calls weren't coming through. As challenging as it was, I would ignore him and keep walking in the opposite direction. I knew he would never go as far as to run up to me and try to physically stop me from ignoring him because he would never want to get caught being desperate in front of his peers. One day while at school, he and one of his male friends were walking behind me. His male friend asked the question, "Don't you still mess with that joint?" Terrence knew that I could hear their conversation, and he replied, "Yeah, she is just in one of her moods." Little did he know, I was determined to show him that I was serious. I was tired of being a revolving door to Terrence. This time I was leaving him for good, and I was not going to recant on my word. Plus, my Mentor was constantly tracking my progress. I did not want to let Jessica down after all the hard work and advice she had invested in me. Nights without Terrence were the hardest. At night, I would get lonely and Terrence would be the only person that seemed to flood my mind. One night, I gave into the urge to see what his life was like without me and I unblocked him on social media. After scrolling through his pictures and postings, I quickly realized for the billionth time the reason why I needed to let him go. Nothing had changed with him. When it came to the process of moving on without Terrence, hours felt like days and days felt like weeks but I knew the process was bettering me. After a month successfully being without Terrence, I celebrated! This was the longest time I had ever gone without giving in and talking to

Terrence. I now realized that living without Terrence was possible. Having Terrence blocked and ignoring him while in public were two of the best strategies that extremely aided the process of moving on. I was very thankful that my Mentor had suggested them to me. I also remembered how Jessica instructed me to use my idle time to explore my unique self and purpose. I made up in my mind that this was exactly what I was going to do. At the time, I was coming to the end of my sophomore year in high school. My grades were poor due to my lack of focus in school and unfortunately for me, the year was coming to an end in less than a few months; which presented me little time to correct my poor academic decisions. Despite the end of the academic year approaching, I was determined that I would begin to put my best foot forward academically. Surprisingly within that short amount of time, my teachers saw a positive change in me. They applauded me for the positive academic change. When it came to my school work, my classes and workload were never challenging. It was just that throughout my high school career, I was never truly interested in applying myself academically.

One of the best parts though about school coming to an end was that Terrence would be graduating in a couple of days, and I would no longer have to see him at school any more. Once school ended, I left with a mindset determined to strive even more my junior year in high school. I desired to pull up my poor grades and GPA (grade point average). By this time, I was three months into the process of moving on and being without Terrence. I figured that since school would be out, it would be even easier to move on from our relationship, since I would no longer have to see him on a consistent basis. Over the summer, I spent my time getting to know myself. I made a list of goals I wanted to pursue after high school; which was to attend college and pursue a law degree. As a young girl, I always dreamed of being a lawyer when I grew up and it was my dream to attend Harvard University for law school. I figured that attending Harvard University was most likely out of the picture due to my lack of academic discipline while in high school so far, so I decided that I would research other colleges that I could attend. It felt like for the first time in a while that things in my life were at peace. Yes, it hurt to move on, but I knew that letting go of Terrence was the best decision I could have made.

Also, regularly attending my church assisted in healing the mental and emotional wounds that resided after the end of Terrence and I's relationship. While on summer break, I avoided places and neighborhoods that reminded me of Terrence. I had come too far to give up and go back to Terrence. I did, however see Terrence and his friends on a few different occasions over the summer, while at the mall. Every time I saw him, a nervousness would come over me and my emotions would start to get out of whack. I would go in the opposite direction or walk on the opposite side of the mall to avoid him. I would try to never look him in the face because I knew if I did, he could easily look at me with his enticing smile and I would have an urge to go back; but since I had already come this far without Terrence, I was determined no matter how hard it was to not go back. I also used my time on summer break to work on ending a few of the habits that I knew were not beneficial to me. I stopped smoking weed and I cut back on partying with friends. It was much easier to let go of these habits considering that many of them I only did for attention or to ease my mind. And since I had deleted one of my biggest stressors, Terrence, I was able to let go of those things too. Ending the relationship with Terrence showed me that I really did have the power to change certain circumstances within in my life. I would have never thought that I would be able to go without Terrence this long but I had, so that showed me that I was able to do the same with other situations within my life. Within the summer, I had days where the loneliness of being without Terrence hit hard. I would see other couples out and about enjoying the joys of being in relationship and it would upset me. Why couldn't I be happy? At times, I thought about entering a new relationship, since it seemed to be plenty of other guys that were interested in me, but I knew that if I was to do so without properly healing, I would be in that relationship to fill my emptiness and not for love.

Life Lesson: Many times, we think that entering another relationship will heal our broken pieces but that is absolutely false. Entering another relationship before you have healed from a prior relationship does more harm than good. It causes you to enter a relationship with trust issues, insecurities, and more. No one should have to take the blame or deal with your past hurt from someone else's actions. Just like you would want to be treated right when you enter a new relationship, someone else would too. Regardless of if that individual says that they are willing to deal with your past hurt and trust issues, it is honestly selfish of you to allow them to do so. They should not have to sign up to carry your extra baggage. Be considerate and take time to properly heal. If many of us would take time to properly heal, we would not find ourselves in situations where we are accumulating broken pieces from one relationship to the next.

Once the summer came to an end, and I began my junior year of high school, I was determined to enter this new academic year with a new mindset. I wanted to leave my past in my past and focus on my future. Since Terrence had graduated, focusing on my schoolwork while at school became much easier. I spent a lot of my time hanging with my friends to aid moving on from Terrence. It was typical of me to regularly go over my friends' houses; however, we would now go on more positive outings, such as going out to dinner and sporting events. My friends knew that when I came over, being cooped up in the house was the last thing I needed, so they made it their duty to take me out and do things I enjoyed. I loved them for that. They knew how hard it was for me to move on from Terrence and ever since I had made the decision to move on they had been supporting me through the entire process. I appreciated their support more than they knew. Of my two closest friends, one of them was named Sidney. Sidney and I had been friends for nearly our entire lives it felt like. Sidney was persistent about making sure I did not hear about or find myself talking about Terrence. She longed for me to move on because she knew I deserved better. She went out her way to keep me occupied and my mind off Terrence. I appreciated her so much. My other friend, Naomi was different. Sidney and Naomi were not close friends. They were merely acquaintances, and the main reason they associated with each other was because of their mutual friendship with me. Naomi supported me leaving Terrence, but she would constantly tell me about what Terrence was doing and whom he was dating next. I knew that constantly hearing about Terrence would do nothing to help me move on but I secretly wanted to know how things were with him. Although he was still doing the same things as far as cheating around with several girls, I privately enjoyed knowing. Another reason Naomi stayed telling me about Terrence was because she dated Terrence's cousin Slim. Naomi and Slim had been together a little over a year. Naomi faced similar issues with Slim as I had with Terrence as far as cheating, but Naomi loved Slim way too much to ever leave him. Slim's cheating was nothing to her. She had practically become numb to his cheating and every time she caught him cheating she would find a way to make it seem as if he was not at fault. She would instead become mad with the girl he was caught cheating with.

Life Lesson: Cheating should not be tolerated in any relationship. It is very important to realize that for one to cheat, an individual must come to the realization that what he/she are doing is wrong and yet despite that realization he/she continues to actively pursue another person whether through conversation, body gestures, sex, etc. If you are currently being cheated on or have been cheated on in the past, it is very important that you realize that it is not solely the fault of the person your significant other cheated with but also the fault of your significant other. Your significant other was well aware of you and their relationship; however, despite that, they decided to cheat and pursue someone else any way.

One day my friend Sidney and I got into an argument. Typically, when we had disagreements, we would quickly resolve the situation since we had been friends for so long. However, this time we did not resolve the conflict. We both had so many people in our ear telling us what they thought we should do, that we ignored what we knew was best to do. The conflict continued to fester to the point where we were no longer speaking to each other. When we would see each other in public we would go in separate directions. As it grew to this point, my other friends that were a part of Sidney and I's clique began to take her side and all of them except one stopped talking to me entirely. The fact that Sidney and I had allowed a small disagreement to cause us to become so distant hurt, but at this point we were both too proud to apologize and make things right. This continued for weeks. During this time, my other friend Naomi and I grew close, and I would spend a lot of time over Naomi's house. All Naomi did was talk about Slim when I was around. I wondered if she ever thought about how talking about Slim affected me, but I never asked. In those moments was when I realized how much I missed Sidney and I's friendship. Sidney and I would always do things together that aided the process of me moving on from Terrence but Naomi did the opposite. One night, Naomi and I decided to go to a football game. Naomi had plans to meet up with Slim at the game, and I decided that when she went off with Slim that I would go sit alone and enjoy the game within the stands. Before leaving from Naomi's house to go to the game, something in my gut told me that Terrence would be at the game and that I should not go. I ignored the feeling and suggested to myself that if I saw him, I would be strong enough to avoid and ignore him. As Naomi and I arrived on the scene of the game everything seemed fine. We walked around the stadium for a while, greeted friends, laughed, bought food from the concession stand, and then found our seats. Shortly after being seated, Naomi received a text from Slim stating that he had just arrived at the game. Naomi looked at me with the biggest smile and told me that Slim was finally here and she wanted to go meet him. I told her to go on and meet him, and that I would be sitting in the same place watching the game once she got back. She explained to me how she did not want to walk through the stadium alone and she asked me if I would come with her to meet Slim. I told her no, but she insisted that I come. I honestly was not too interested in watching the game; however, I knew that staying put in the stands would keep me from running into Terrence. After debating in my mind on what to do, I decided that I would walk with her to meet Slim and come straight back to my seat. Then, Naomi and I got up from our seats and headed to meet Slim. As we approached Slim, I noticed a tall, skinny, dark skinned guy standing beside him. The closer we got, I realized who it was. My stomach got tight and I wished that I would have simply stayed in my seat in the stands. Terrence peered around Slim and smiled at me. Was this a set up? Why was he smiling? Was he that prideful to think that after six months of being on my own, I would be here to see him? Once Naomi and I got to where they were standing, Naomi greeted Slim and Terrence. I spoke only to Slim. Once Naomi felt comfortable with Slim, I told her that I was leaving and going back to my seat. As I was speaking those words to Naomi, Terrence attempted to cut me off by saying flirtatious remarks about how I needed to stay over there with him. Naomi could tell by my face that I felt uncomfortable and she told Slim that she would catch up with him later that night and asked if I was ready to head back to our seats. Once we got back to our seats, all I could think about were the comments Terrence said to me. I wanted to push them out my mind, but they secretly aroused me and I was covertly happy that he missed me.

Once the game was over, Naomi asked if I could stop her by Slim's house for a few minutes and I said yes. Once we got there, I figured she would be in there for a while, so I decided to come inside as well. Once we walked through the door, there stood Slim and Terrence. My stomach instantly felt queasy. Naomi and I entered the living room and sat down on the couch. Slim came and set down beside Naomi and Terrence went into another room. I was glad Terrence was gone. I privately wanted to go back to the car but a voice in my head told me that going back to the car would make me look weak. So, I continued sitting on the sofa. About ten minutes passed and Slim and Naomi left and went into another room. I already knew what was getting ready to take place between Slim and Naomi. She and Slim were about to get it in. About five more minutes passed and Terrence came out of the other room. My stomach dropped! I knew it would be extremely hard for me to ignore Terrence while alone with him in this room. He came over and sat down beside me. It was like I wanted him there but I knew I did not need him there. He scooted near me and smiled. Then he reached over and put one of his hands on my leg, and in that moment, we both wanted the same thing. I could not fight the temptation any longer and we kissed for the first time in over six months. He got up and told me to come with him into this other room. We entered a pitch-black room, and he sat down on a bed, and signaled for me to come closer. I stood in front of him and we kissed. Everything felt so wrong but I wanted it so bad. It was like my mind was telling me no but my body was telling me yes. He tugged on my jeans and unbuttoned my pants. Once they were unbuttoned, he started to pull them down but I interrupted him by saying, "No." He looked up at me with a smile and started to feel all over me and he asked me if I was sure I wanted him to stop. His touch felt so good and I missed it so much. I gave in and we had sex.

Life Lesson: Be careful who you hang around. Your "crew" or group of friends has more of an effect on you than you think. If you hang with a group of people that do not value themselves, although you may think it will not change your perspective of yourself, slowly but surely, you will see their values reflected in your actions. Think about the group of friends that you have now. Do you all act similar? Whether you realize it or not, the people you spend the majority of your time with influence your actions and decision making. Therefore, it is so important to surround yourself with friends who are going in the direction you want to pursue. If you want to be financially secure, spend a lot of your time around people who know how to save and budget. I am not saying to ditch your old friends, but prioritize your life to the point where you spend more time with the people that reflect the character traits you aspire to develop versus the ones you do not. Now do not get me wrong, sometimes to do this, it may require you to unfriend a friend or two but keep in mind that you are making hard decisions now for a better future later. I am not for one second saying that surrounding yourself with people that reflect the qualities that you aspire to have will be comfortable.

*It most cases, doing so will be uncomfortable. At times, you may feel like compared to them you are not good enough, but remember to never compare yourself but instead soak up all the knowledge you possibly can. **#Checkyourcircle.***

After Naomi and I left Slim's place, I drove Naomi to her house. The conversation during the ride was nearly silent. Naomi would try to spark conversation, but I kept it short. All that was going through my mind was how stupid I was to have had sex with Terrence again. I felt so hurt; I just wanted to cry. How could I have been so stupid? How could I go six months without Terrence to go directly back to him again? I felt like the entire process of me moving on was now void. There would be no way Terrence would take me serious after this and if my Mentor was to know about this incident, she would be so disappointed. So many emotions flooded my mind. Once we got to Naomi's house, I dropped her directly off and hurried home. The conviction of knowing what I did was so wrong devastated me. I knew God was not pleased and I did not know if God would forgive me for this. There was absolutely no excuse for what happened at Slim's. I knew that what I was doing was wrong but I persisted. I felt as if I deserved to have Terrence not take me serious after this incident. After tossing and turning all night with this on my mind, I finally ended up drifting off to sleep. The next morning, I woke up determined to let Terrence know that despite what happened that prior night, our dealings and relationship was still over. Once I arrived at school that morning, while in my morning Health class, I drafted up a detailed message to Terrence. I remembered that before I could send a message to Terrence I had to unblock him, so I did. After I unblocked Terrence on my cell phone, a message came through from him about how much he enjoyed last night. I texted him back explaining to him how I had not planned for that to happen and that I was not happy it took place. He replied to me saying how I apparently wanted it to happen by the actions I displayed to him last night. I knew this conversation needed to end, so I sent him the multiple paragraph message that I had spent all morning drafting up. Once I sent the message, I blocked him back and deleted our conversation thread from my phone. This time around, I was not concerned with what his response would be to the final message I sent him. I was officially done with him for good this time. After I handled my dealing with Terrence, all I could think about was Naomi and how bad of a friend she was to even encourage me to go around Terrence when she knew I was trying to move on. Sidney would have never allowed such. Of course, it was my fault that everything that happened took place, but I felt as if she was a real friend that truly cared about my mental and emotional well-being she would not have put me in such a predicament. I decided that it would be best to distance myself from Naomi for a while. Although I had sent the message to Terrence and decided to take my distance from Naomi, it did not cause the conviction of my actions to fade. I still carried around the disappointment that I had let down myself, my mentor, and most importantly God. As the weeks went by, my life felt so lonely. I had lost my best friend Sidney because of an immature argument, my other friends had nearly abandoned me, Naomi and I were taking our distance, Terrence was officially out of the picture, and I felt left alone with no one to turn to. Despite how I felt, I let my hurt fuel me to keep pushing.

Life Lesson: Often times we would rather waddle in our sorrow than use our obstacles to motivate us to do better and achieve greater. Just because you made a mistake does not mean it is the end of the world. I am not saying that you should not hold yourself to a certain standard, but do not allow your mistakes to cause you to feel depressed and beneath anyone. Maybe you had a bad day, which is not a reason to believe that you have a bad life. Refocus your mind; things will get better. They always do when we decide not to focus on our obstacles but instead allow them to motivate us for the better.

Before I knew it, it was the second week of December and we were receiving our academic report cards. In a few days, school would be coming to an end for Christmas break. Once I received my report card, I was a bit nervous to open it. This was going to be my first report card of my junior year. I opened it and to my surprise for the first time in my entire life I had straight "A's." I could not believe it. The biggest smile took over my entire face. I took a picture of my report card and sent it to nearly everyone including my family members, friends, my Mentor, and a few of my church friends. I most importantly, thanked God because without Him this would not have been possible. I felt so relieved to know that my recent slip up with Terrence did not cause me to decline academically. After reading all the positive responses I received from my family and friends about my report card, I literally felt the happiest I had in months. I knew that if I could make straight A's this one time, I had it in me to make it a continuous habit.

Chapter Six
Second Place

*M*y first day back to school once Christmas break concluded was difficult. I still was getting use to the process of learning how to function independent from my regular group of friends. My normal clique of friends were still acting distant towards me because of Sidney and I's disagreement. And Naomi and I were still taking our distance apart from one other due to the issue I had with her regarding Terrence. At times, I felt so lonely walking through the hallways and eating lunch alone. After enduring several weeks of being extremely isolated at school, I began to mingle and make friends with two individuals named Chelsea and Dominque. My days were much more enjoyable with Chelsea and Dominique by my side. Easily, we created a bond and friendship to where we would hang together nearly every day at school. When away from each other, Chelsea, Dominque, and I would communicate through group text messages. The more time I spent with them the better I felt. It was as if I was given a fresh start when it came to building friendships. My friend Dominque worked a lot during the week and on the weekends, so for the most part Chelsea and I spent the most time together over the weekend. Chelsea also had a brother name Christopher who went to school with us as well. Christopher was a year older than I and since I would go over Chelsea's house regularly, I would always end up seeing Christopher. Often times, when I would hang out over Chelsea's house, Chelsea, Christopher, Christopher's friends, and I would all end of hanging together. Christopher was a nice guy. He was athletic and had a tremendously outgoing personality. He was very sociable and many of his friends referred to him as the "go-to" guy for advice. I personally did not feel comfortable going to Christopher for advice when recommended at first since Christopher and I were not technically friends, but after spending a lot time with Christopher while over his sister's house, we practically became friends too. We eventually exchanged numbers, and we would talk from time to time through text messages. I never mingled too close with Christopher though, because he had a girlfriend. He and his girlfriend had been dating for a while now and their relationship status was serious. The last thing I needed in my life was guy drama. I had dealt with that so much while with Terrence that at this point I was determined to make it my business to avoid getting involved in any more guy drama with anyone else.

One day, while carrying the weight of the heartbreak from Terrence and I's relationship, I decided that I would confide in Christopher and get his advice on my past relationship with Terrance. I wanted to know what he would suggest I do moving forward. I wanted Christopher's opinion on whether I should pursue another relationship or wait for Terrence to get his act together. Although I knew Terrence was no good for me, I reasoned with myself that he may not be good for me now, but maybe later Terrence and I could try being in a relationship again.

Life Lesson: Never wait on a man to change. When we are blinded by love, we think it is ideal for us to simply put our relationship life on hold and wait for someone to grow up, mature or change. Yet this perception is completely invalid. It is important that you realize your worth as an individual. No matter how much you may believe you love an individual, you must realize that your time is more valuable than to wait on someone else to change. If the individual cannot respect you now, what makes you think that they deserve for you to wait on them to do so later? Also, while you are waiting for them to mature there is no guarantee that they will actually indeed change. Sometimes we fall in love with the potential someone has. We reason with ourselves by saying, "They have the potential to be a good partner. They have the potential to be a good father. They have the potential to change." Yes, they may have the potential to do so, but that does not mean they will. Always remember that potential is not promised. Therefore, just because someone has the potential to do something, does not mean that they will actually fulfill the promise, duty or standard.

After sharing with Christopher the details of my past relationship with Terrence, he comforted me by telling me that I was worth more than having Terrence treat me the way he did. He told me that I deserved better and that I should not go back to Terrence. Hearing Christopher say those words made me feel so redeemed. I had been with Terrence for so long and had dealt with his repetitive ways for so long that I had forgot that I actually deserved better. I also shared with Christopher how I desired to be treated in a relationship moving forward and I longed to know whether my desires of being treated respectfully and given adequate attention were obtainable within a relationship. He assured me that everything I desired was realistic and achievable. After talking with Christopher, I felt so relieved to know that what I anticipated out of a relationship was attainable. After that day of confiding in Christopher, our friendship grew even closer. After feeling how genuine Christopher's advice was, I now felt more comfortable to confide in him the more. A few days after our conversation, while reflecting on what we had discussed, I concluded that I was going to take a break from dating and relationships. I was tired of being placed in second place to another woman and I figured one way to put an end to that would be to stop dating completely until I felt confident in someone enough to start dating again. I decided that I would instead continue to strive academically and allow my academics to be my focus. I had already wasted enough time academically on boys. With next year being my senior year, I had no more time to waste on distractions. I had been successfully acing my goal of achieving straight A's throughout my junior year and I was determined to finish off this last semester of my junior year with nothing less than straight A's. One day while researching colleges I could attend post high school graduation, I came across an ad to spend a summer at Harvard University. I read through the details of the ad, and it explained that Harvard University was offering a seven week pre-collegiate summer intensive program offering high school students the opportunity to spend a summer at Harvard and earn college credits while studying a major of their choice. I thought to myself how this was such an amazing opportunity, yet I most likely would not be able to attend because of my poor academic record my freshman and sophomore year of high school. Once I finished reading the details, I scrolled passed the ad, and went back to my college research. After a few minutes went by, I scrolled back to the ad. I reread the details of the ad over and over until I finally decided to click on the ad and view more information. Once I clicked the ad, it took me to a webpage to complete an enrollment application. The webpage stated that the deadline to submit your application was the next week. Above the application, following the basic instructions, stated in bold letters, **"Applicants can be denied."** I felt as if my heart skipped a beat for a second. I hesitantly began to scroll through the application requirements. I debated back and forth to myself on whether I should complete the application. I then decided to call my academic mentor and share with him the details of this opportunity and ask him if I should apply. Once I called him and shared with him the details, he unwavering stated to me how this was an outstanding opportunity and that I should apply. I took his advice and completed the application. Once I completed the application, I received an email stating that my application was being processed and I would hear something back by March 20th, which was four weeks away.

While waiting to hear back from Harvard's Admission Board, my friendship with Christopher continued to flourish. We had been talking to each other nearly every day since the day I had confided in him about Terrence. We would plan times to hang out together as friends, and the more time we spent getting to know each other as friends, the closer we became. At times, I did not go over Chelsea's house to see her, but to see Christopher. After about a week or two passed, our interaction shifted. Our causal laughs would end with flirtatious comments, and our conversational hugs would lead to sensual touches. I was not quite sure what was taking place between Christopher and I, but I did not try to stop the attention I was receiving either. It was as if he had noted everything that I had said I desired in a guy and he began to pursue me in those very same ways that I had expressed. I knew that everything that was taking place between Christopher and I was going against his current relationship, yet Christopher was aware of that fact too; meanwhile, he continued to pursue me. At times when guilt would try to seep in, I would reason with myself into feeling less blameworthy because it was not as if I was the only one who was aware of their actions. Even though I was aware that Christopher had a girlfriend, at times I did not mind being his side chick. The way he treated me was much better than Terrence had, so if being his side chick was what I would have to be considered to get treated the way I desired, then so be it. Christopher made me feel so special. The conversations that we shared between each other were like no other. It was as if I was finally being shown the individualized love and attention that I wanted out of a relationship. One weekend, I ended up spending the entire weekend over Chelsea's house, and while I was over there, Christopher and I stayed cuddled up the entire time. I figured Chelsea and Christopher's friends respected our side relationship because they never bothered to say anything to us about it. One night during that specific weekend, while cuddled up with Christopher, one hand gesture led to another, and without a doubt Christopher and I ended up having sex for the first time. After we had sex, everything felt so casual as if we had had sex before. At first, I felt slightly convicted about having sex with Christopher because I knew that God was not pleased with having sex outside of marriage, but since I was not having sex with Terrence again, I felt that this time would be looked at differently. Christopher treated me right. Yes, he had a girlfriend which was wrong, but everything else felt subsequently right. Our private relationship behind the scenes went on for about three weeks until I concluded that Christopher should end the relationship with his girlfriend. Christopher and his girlfriend had been dating for almost a year but Christopher's girlfriend was young, immature, and closed-minded. I figured that with her he was settling and for him to leave her for me would be his gain. I offered him so much more than a pretty face and a nice body. I offered him that plus more and he knew it. After drafting up the idea in my head of Christopher leaving his girlfriend, I decided that I would present the idea to him. I did not want to present it to him in such a manner that reflected the fact that I thought his girlfriend was inadequate, but instead I wanted to ask him if he saw a future between us, and when he said he did, I would suggest to him that he should leave his girlfriend.

Life Lesson: It is never okay to try to break up someone else's relationship for your own selfish greed and gain. Although you may think the relationship is already on bad terms or needs to come to an end, it is not your job to end it. Just because someone's relationship looks hopeless does not mean you need to step in and orchestrate the direction it goes in next.

God does not honor that and just the way you claim to have taken him from someone else, he could easily be taken away from you. Be careful of the seeds you sow.

One night while texting Christopher over the phone, I sent him a message regarding whether he saw a future in our relationship. Christopher responded back saying how we were simply friends with benefits. Reading those words, reminded me of how I used to ask Terrence about our relationship status and he would respond in a lessening manner. Completely torn by Christopher's response, I was not sure what to do. How could we just be friends with benefits? Of course, I did not mind being Christopher's side boo in the beginning, but since more than just my confided secrets but my sex and my emotions were involved, how we could just be "friends with benefits" was mind boggling. Was I not more to him than a friend who he was also sleeping with? I was complexed because the way he treated me reflected more than simply friends with benefits. Christopher and I had never exchanged intimate words like "I love you" but I knew that someway and somehow his feelings went beyond just friends with benefits. I responded back to Christopher by saying, "Okay," even though I was truly heartbroken inside. The next day, I did not hear from Christopher all morning. I felt that despite the response I had given him that night, he knew that I was upset with his response. I finally heard from him later that day and we engaged in a brief casual conversation. Although I was upset with Christopher, I still wanted to see him. While at school, I talked to his sister Chelsea about coming to her house after school. She said I could come over for a little while but once her mom got home I would have to leave because they were going shopping that evening for a special occasion. I told her that I understood and that it was fine, and that I did not mind hanging with her even if it was only for a little while. Secretly, I did not want to hang out with her, I really wanted to see Christopher. Once we got to her house, I saw Christopher. I did not show it publicly, but my entire mood brightened by seeing Christopher. While I was with Chelsea upstairs in her room, Christopher and I texted back and forth the entire time. Christopher and I came up with a plan that once his mother got home and his mother and sister left, I could come back and spend time with him since he would have the entire house to himself until they got back that evening. So, once Chelsea's mom got home, Chelsea told me that I had to go and that she would talk to me later and see me tomorrow at school. Once I left out of their house, I got in my car, drove around the block and waited. After about ten minutes, Christopher texted me and told me that his mother and sister had left and that I could come back. I drove back around the block and parked back where I had parked initially. I figured, I would not be over Christopher's house long, so it would be fine for me to park back in the same spot. Once I got to the door, Christopher opened the door and told me to come inside. Once inside, we both smiled at each other and Christopher led me downstairs to his room. We engaged in small talk, and before I knew it I was stretch out on Christopher bed. For the second time, we had sex. After we had sex, we both got dressed, talked and watched a little television. After about fifteen minutes, I felt as if we were simply going through the motions and I left. This time when I left his house, I knew for sure that everything that had been going on between Christopher and I over the past month and a half was strictly lust and not love.

Life Lesson: Lust is when we are strongly drawn to people or things because of our sexual desires outside the context of marriage. (If you are married, it is not a sin to be sexually drawn to your spouse.) Sometimes we fail to realize the difference between love and lust. Anytime, a relationship is centered around sex (outside of marriage), sexual thought or pleasures, nudity, pornography, etc., nine times out of ten the relationship is or is being built on lust. Also, it is possible for you to love someone, yet have your relationship still built on lust. The foundation of any relationship should be built and centered on God, and after God it should be founded on friendship, trust, honesty, and security. When your relationship is instead founded on nude photos or sex; meaning those were one of the first things you all did or engaged in in the beginning of your relationship, chances are your relationship is built on lust and not love.

After I concluded that our relationship was built on lust and not love, I began to realize how the last month and a half of my life was a complete waste. I did not realize it then but I now realized that my relationship with Christopher was a repeat of my past relationship with

Terrance. Although Christopher treated me much better than Terrence, the underlying issue was still the same. I was still being put in second place by a man to another woman. Although it hurt to come to that realization, it became clearer to me that that was what had been taking place. Christopher had a girlfriend and despite whether I thought they should be together — he still had a girlfriend. And no matter how good he treated me that was not an excuse for me to settle with being his side girl. I hated myself for being so naïve again. Although it did not take me nearly two years like it did with Terrence to realize that it was time to move on, but the very fact that it had taken almost two months alone was still disappointing to me. Why did it seem like I always had the best intentions, yet I always found myself in situations that positioned me in second place? Was I not good enough to be someone's first choice? Was I not pretty enough or smart enough? What was it that kept causing me to be thrown into second place to another woman?

Life Lesson: Be aware of generational curses. What is a generational curse? A generational curse is a negative pattern of behavior that has been passed down from generation to generation. For example, a generational curse could be anger, alcoholism, abuse, pornography, lust, and the list goes on. To put a generational curse into perspective, let's say your great grandmother was an alcoholic, your grandmother was also an alcoholic, your mother is an alcoholic, and now you struggle with alcoholism; that is a prime example. Generational curses can also deal with living conditions. Say your grandfather lived in a poor neighborhood, then your dad raised you in a poor neighborhood, and now you are raising your children in a less fortunate neighborhood. Now you may be saying to yourself, "How is where you raise your children a sin?" It is not. I am more so dealing with the generational curse of the mindset. The generational curse is not where they live but why they live there. For generations, no one has successfully shifted to better living conditions. The enemy uses generational curses to keep you living and behaving below the means of where God has called you to be. The enemy wants that alcohol addiction that caused your mom to not achieve to her fullest potential to stop you from achieving to your fullest potential. The enemy wants that pornography addiction that kept *your father and grandfather from being in a stable relationship to cause you not to be able to maintain a stable relationship also. Throughout my life I have had to face and overcome many generational curses. One of the main ones was allowing oneself to settle with being second place to another woman while in a relationship. For several generations, many individuals within my family have dated married men and have even had children by married men. Others have settled with men that continuously cheat, all because they fail to realize their worth. The great thing about generational curses is that they can be broken through Jesus! There is no generational curse that is stronger than the power of Jesus and through God you can break any generational curse that Satan has put over you and your family.*

I had a few days left until I would hear back from Harvard's Admissions Board, and my nerves were all over the place. I nervously checked my email several times a day to see if the Admissions Board had possibly emailed me earlier with their decision. I assured myself that if this opportunity was for me, I would be accepted and if not, I would still be okay. I did not want to put too much of my hope into this opportunity with the likelihood that I may not be accepted. The following day, with only three days left until I would hear back from Harvard, my high school principal stopped by my classroom and asked to speak with me. Once the principal and I were out of the classroom, he asked me if I was aware that I did not get accepted into the Harvard program because of my academic & behavior records. In that moment, it felt as if my heart had shattered into a thousand pieces. I nodded yes, although I really had not found out yet, but I wanted to hear what else he had to say. He went on to inform me that once he received the call from Harvard's Admission Board that day regarding my results, he informed me that while on the phone with them, he had shared with them how much I had matured and developed and in response the Admissions Board wanted to speak with me over the phone upstairs in his office. I could not believe what I had heard. Did my principal just say that the Admissions Board was on the line upstairs waiting to speak with me? Panicking, I asked my principal what I should say to them on the phone. He told me that the Admissions Board had denied me because of a suspension from my freshman year that I had on my behavioral record. He said that the board wants to hear for themselves my growth and development. He then asked me if I was ready to proceed upstairs. I told him that I was ready and we walked upstairs to his office. Once in his office, he directed me to the phone and told me that they were on the line. I nervously picked up the phone and said, "Hello." While on the phone with the Admissions Board, they asked me several questions concerning my suspension my freshman year and my poor academic performance throughout high school. I truthfully explained to them how I was very distracted my freshman and sophomore year with negative influences. Once the conversation concluded, they informed me that they would contact me via email regarding my acceptance. Once I got off the phone, my principal asked me how I thought the conversation went and I shared with him that I had been honest with the board and that I believe that it had went well. I then thanked him for believing in me enough to inform the Admissions Board of my growth. If it was not for him, they would have not even thought to give me a second chance.

Life Lesson: Everything that you do in life has a consequence whether it be good or bad. Always think of the consequences before you make your decisions. In this case, an argument that had caused me to get suspended was on the verge of declining me from an academic opportunity to attend the school of my dreams for the summer. If it was not for God using my principal in that moment, I would not have even been afforded the opportunity to explain myself to the Admissions Board over the phone. Often times we fail to realize the consequences of our actions until it is too late. The same applies spiritually. Once you commit a sin, there is still a consequence. Yes, you may have repented and God forgave you, but there will still be a consequence of some sort due to your actions. Maybe you fornicated, and repented but you still ended up getting pregnant and having a baby you were not ready for. Maybe you lied, and because of that lie it broke up your friendship with someone. Repentance does not remove the consequence but it instead allows God to show you grace within the consequence. So instead of God allowing the very worst to happen to you because of your decision, He shows you grace and gives you a consequence that is less than the severity of your decision. I thank God for His grace, because without His grace and redirection, I would not be the woman I am now.

On the morning of March, the 20th, I checked my email nearly every five minutes awaiting the response of Harvard's Admissions Board. Several hours went by without receiving a single response from the board. I began to questionably wonder why I had not received a response yet. Could it be that the candidates that were not accepted, were going to be notified last? I knew that it being a Friday, if I did not receive a response from them, the thought of whether I had been accepted or denied would worry me the entire weekend. A few more hours went by until I decided to check my email again for the zillionth time. It was about five in the evening, and I had concluded that if I had not heard anything from the Admissions Board by then, I would probably not hear from them until Monday. Surprisingly, when I checked my email this final time, there sat an email from the Harvard University Admissions Board. My body nearly froze as I stared at the unread email. I was so nervous to actually open and read my application results. I had waited anxiously over the past four weeks waiting to hear back, yet I had the decision at my fingertips and I felt paralyzed to find out my results. I debated on whether I should read the email now or wait until late that evening to read it. What was I going to do if I was not accepted? Would I cry or would I just brush it off? I was not sure of my own reaction at this point. I reassured myself as I had before that if this opportunity was for me that I would get accepted and if not, that did not mean it was the end of the world. More opportunities would cross my path. I finally decided to open the email. As I read the email, tears began to form in my eyes. I could not believe it. I had got accepted into the program! Was this a dream? I forwarded the email to my mom and academic mentor. I could not believe what I had just read. I had been accepted to attend Harvard University for the summer. After sharing with my family, friends and academic mentor my results, I decided to post my acceptance on social media. I posted on Facebook about my acceptance and tons of people congratulated me. Over the next few weeks, every time I turned around someone was congratulating me on my acceptance. It at times felt unreal. I was even contacted by two news reporters who wanted to do stories on my acceptance into Harvard University for the summer. One news reporter was a reporter for a local news station and the other was a journalist for our local newspaper. I could not believe all the spotlight I was receiving from the acceptance. I knew attending Harvard for the summer was a huge opportunity, yet I was not quite sure how I felt about receiving all the attention and spotlight. At first, having pictures taken of me for the news and receiving all the congratulations felt amazing, but I later felt as if I was truly living a lie. People were complimenting me on my growth, but had I really matured and grown up? No one knew the real me who was unsure of her worth. The true me who was just sleeping around with someone else's man two weeks ago. The girl that was still trying to get over her Ex, and still battling with low self-esteem. Everyone just saw the Harvard acceptance and my recent academic performance and assumed I was perfect.

Life Lesson: Just because an individual looks the part does not mean that they truly are who they display. Just because someone looks happy does not mean that they are not broken. Stop comparing your life to someone else's highlights. Stop examining all the spotlight someone else is receiving and assume that they have it all together. We compare ourselves to the success stories of others not knowing what issues, disappointments, failures, grief, and various other obstacles they may have had to face. Stop trying to measure up to the image that someone else displays. Remember it is a display, meaning that someone else is on the other side. Whether or not who the individual displays is the real them is between them and God, but stop comparing yourself to someone else as if they are flawless. We all face issues, insecurities, and situations. Comparing yourself to others only stunts your growth. Remain focused on who God is grooming you to be because what people display is not always what or how they truly live.

Chapter 7
Change

*A*long with being accepted into the Harvard University Summer Intensive Program, I was also awarded a scholarship of $6,000 to attend the program from the college. Considering my family's current financial state, the college would have offered me more financial support; however, since I had applied so close to the deadline the college's scholarship fund for the program was at its max. The total cost to attend the program at Harvard University was $11,000, so my family and I were left with $5,000 to raise in less than three months. Fortunately, due to the various media outlets featuring my acceptance story, I had a community of supporters that generously gave towards the remaining balance of my tuition. I would be out in public, and individuals would recognize me from the newspaper or news station and would write generous checks as donations towards the remaining balance of my tuition. One in particular organization invited me to attend their annual banquet event, where they publicly presented me with a check to use towards the cost of my tuition. The support I received was extremely warming and it left my family with very little money to gather up on our own. Also, when I informed my then Pastor of the news of my acceptance, he also helped me raise funds by encouraging his congregation of nearly three hundred people to help sponsor my trip. While in the mist of fundraising and preparing to leave for Harvard in June, which was only a month away, a guy named Justin, reached out to me asking if he could take me out on a date. I had remembered initially meeting Justin a year ago, in passing one day at our local mall. I had also remembered how he had randomly asked me to go to prom with him earlier this year; however, I had declined due to my fling with Christopher. Yet this guy persistently continued to reach out to me on social media, despite how many times I ignored him. And now here he was again, reaching out to me on Facebook, yet this time he asked me if he could take me out on a date. I declined his date offer because to be honest, at this point, I was so done with relationships. It seemed as if every relationship I entered fell through and I was tired of having my heart broken over and over. Plus, Justin was not my type at all. He was the opposite of what I wanted appearance wise in a man. He was short, a non-athlete, too proper, and seemed to come across as a push over. The very fact that he had asked me on a date was odd. I had never been asked on a date before.

Life Lesson: Often times when we are so used to frequently settling for less in relationships, we find it hard to accept or acknowledge when someone actually approaches us with the right approach or wants to treat us right because we are so used to being treated in a devalued manner. Beware of pushing away those who treat you positively different. You'll miss out on the individual God has for you by chasing after the characteristics of the individuals of your past relationships.

Even after declining Justin's date offer, he continued to pursue me. He would send me polite and gentle messages through Facebook, wishing me to have a great day or to have a great week. He was so well mannered and respectful that it was honestly strange. I was so used to guys telling me how sexy I was or after knowing them for only two weeks going over their house to "chill," yet this guy was completely different. It seemed as if he was more interested in getting to know me personally versus indulging in my physical appearance. At the time, school had just ended and I had only three weeks left until I would be leaving for Harvard. Thankfully, my family and I were finally able to raise the outstanding balance for my tuition. The only thing I had left to do to prepare for Harvard was to purchase dorm supplies, personal care and hygiene products, and a few other miscellaneous items to prepare for my life in Cambridge, Massachusetts for the next seven weeks. I was nearly ecstatic to have the opportunity to study at Harvard University for the summer, yet I was extremely nervous to be twelve hours away from my family and friends for over a month's time. With little left to do in preparation of the seven-week Summer Intensive Program at Harvard, I decided that I would give Justin a chance and take up his date offer. Nearly two weeks had already passed since he had asked me. That day, I sent him a message asking him if he was still interested in going out on the date. He eagerly informed me that he was and he asked if I could meet him in an hour at Olive Garden. I was already formally dressed as I was invited to attend a church service that evening where I would be given the opportunity to speak to about my acceptance to Harvard and ask for donations. I knew it would take me little to no time to freshen up and drive to Olive Garden. We both arrived at Olive Garden at the same time; I was honestly nervous as to what to expect on this date. I had never been on a date before and I had not seen Justin in nearly a year. I opened my car door, and proceeded to walk to the front door of the restaurant. Once I got to the door, Justin opened it for me and escorted me in. Once we got our table, we sat down and began to engage in small talk. He asked me how my day was and how many days I had left until I would be leaving for Harvard. I informed him that I only had two weeks left and he congratulated me on my acceptance. Then he asked what my long-term goal was after attending the Summer Intensive Program at Harvard. I informed him that my long-term goal was to study law and become a lawyer. I shared with him how I wanted to move to Atlanta, Georgia, open my own law firm, purchase my dream home, and live as a single woman for the rest of my life. He looked at me puzzled, I guess concerned with the fact that I bluntly said that

I pretty much had no desire to get married and settle down with someone, yet I was on this date. After I shared with him my plans, he asked me what I believed I was purposed by God to do. I paused for a moment and then I went on to share with him that I believed that the future plans I had shared with him were my purpose. To be honest, no one had ever asked me that question before. I had heard my Pastor talk about being purposed by God to do something; however, I felt as if God had never shared with me what it was that I was purposed to do. I had dreamed of being a lawyer ever since I was a child, so I figured that if that was my dream ever since I was young, that must be my purpose in life. Plus, my entire family supported the idea of me being a lawyer. At the time, no one in my family had successfully completed college and pursued a career, so majority of my family pushed me to be the first one to graduate college and pursue my goals. Once I explained to Justin that I believed being a lawyer and owning my own law firm to be my purpose, he continued to look at me with a blank stare. He asked me if I had ever considered being an empowerment speaker for women or even some sort of mentor to women. I looked at him as if he was crazy. I thought to myself that if this boy knew more about me, he would not be suggesting that I be some sort of example to women. I told him that I had not considered that field. I explained to him that I was content with the goals that I had already mapped out for my future. Justin smiled and then changed the conversation. Our date from that point on proceeded with little to no more questions. I figured Justin had concluded that I was pretty set in my ways and the goals I had put in place for my future were set in stone. I was not going to let anyone change the goals that I had set out to achieve ever since I was a young girl. The date went well as the night went on. Once the date was over, Justin walked me to my car and sent me on my way. All I could think about on my way home was Justin and I's date. Although Justin was not my type physically, his personality was attractive. I had never felt so open while alone with a guy. Justin was actually interested in me as an individual opposed to the other guys I had been with. Justin was different, and I liked that about him. That night Justin sent me a message expressing how much he enjoyed our date. Little did he know, that simple text made my night!

A few days went by and then Justin asked me on another date. Since the prior date had went well, I took this date invitation without hesitation. Our second date took place at a local hot wing spot. Once I arrived at the venue, Justin met me at the front door and opened the door for me and escorted me in. Having the door opened for me made me feel so important. Although, it was a simple gesture, to not have had any guy do that for me before made the small gesture feel so magnified. It was as if Justin was doing so much more than the guys of my past, yet I had not given up anything to Justin at all. We had not had sex or even kissed. We had only been on dates; moreover, I was so amazed by his character. While on our second date, Justin and I talked about a series of topics. He asked questions that allowed him to get to know me more. He asked questions about my family, friends, current job, favorite foods, hobbies, and colors. I loved how interested Justin was in my personal hobbies and experiences. At the end of our date, Justin walked me to my car. As we walked to my car, he expressed to me how although he did not know me as well, he was going to miss me while I was at Harvard. I was leaving for Harvard in less than three days, and although I was not too familiar with Justin, I was going to miss him too. Within just those two dates and simple conversations through text messages, I had already begun to feel a friendship forming between Justin and I. The only issue was that I did not see a future with Justin, yet that was what he desired with me. In that moment, I felt so convicted because Justin was such a sweet guy, yet while on our second date I could barely stay focused on Justin and I's conversation because I was too busy debating in my head about whether I was going to send Terrence a message tonight asking if I could see him before I left for Harvard in three days. Although Terrence and I had not talked in nearly six months, I longed to see him before I left. I had no desire to see Christopher since I knew that our relationship had been centered on nothing but lust and not love. However, I did want to see Terrence before I left and I knew if I texted him asking if I could come over, even though we had not seen each other in nearly six months, he would still allow me to come over without hesitation. When I got to my car, Justin opened my car door for me, and once I sat down inside my car, I rolled down the window to continue conversation with him before I left. I felt as if at the very least, Justin deserved this time to talk with me if I was to make the decision to go see Terrence tonight. As our conversation came to an end, Justin asked a question that shifted the dynamic of our entire conversion. He asked me if I knew that I was his wife! I hesitated for a second and asked him what he meant. He repeated the question again, "Do you know that you are my wife?" I told him that I was not his future wife and that I was not sure where he was getting this crazy idea that I would be his wife from. I expressed to him that he was making me feel uncomfortable by saying such. I put my car in reverse and began to back up with Justin still standing at my window. The thought of him thinking that I was his future wife made me sick to my stomach. I was not interested in being anything more than a friend to Justin. As I was backing up, Justin made another remark that changed my perspective on everything. He said, "And whatever you are planning on doing with someone tonight, do not do it." I stopped the car and looked back at Justin in shock. How did he know what I was planning to do tonight? It was as if God had spoken through Justin in that very moment. With everything appearing to be and sound so strange from Justin, I immediately put my car back in reverse, told him bye, and left the restaurant parking lot. I had heard my Pastor talk about how God could use people to speak to you in certain moments; however, if God had used Justin in that moment, why did God allow for Justin to say that I was his future wife when I was not? I ended up making the decision to not text Terrence that night, and I simply ended up going back home. That night I reflected on how my second date went with Justin and I was not too sure how to feel. I laid in my bed looking up at the ceiling, puzzled, until I finally went off to sleep. The next day, my family and I spent the entire day mapping out our road trip to Harvard. My family decided that while on the way to Harvard, we would stop in Queens, New York and visit family for a few days and then head to Harvard the following Monday morning. Once the arrangements were made, we packed our bags and left town Thursday night, traveling to Queens, New York. Once we arrived at our family's house in Queens, New York on Friday morning, we rested. After we rested for a while, we left the house and went on to explore the city of New York. We visited the Twin Tower exhibit, rode the ferry, shopped, and ate delicious food. After spending the entire day in the city, we headed back to our family's house and enjoyed the evening with them. The following day, which was Saturday, we spent the day enjoying our family. Before I knew it, it was Sunday evening, and we were concluding our stay in Queens, New York and preparing to head to Harvard for check-in. My family and I left early Monday morning to embark on our four-hour drive to Harvard for check-in. As we arrived on the campus of Harvard University, I began to experience mixed emotions; I was extremely excited yet extremely nervous. Once we found parking on campus, we got out and started exploring the campus. I was amazed by the prestige campus building designs. Harvard literally looked exactly like the pictures plus more. Once my family and I arrived at the check in building, my mom helped me get checked in. Once I was given my Harvard ID and dorm key, my family drove me to my dorm and helped me carry in my luggage. Once in my dorm, my family and I reorganized the furniture in my room, put on my bed sheets, stocked my pantry area, opened my brand-new desk supplies, and helped me organize my work study desk. After we finished setting up my dorm, we headed over to the bookstore and purchased my books for my courses, and any additional supplies I needed for class.

We purchased pencils, pens, and notebooks with Harvard embroidery. By the time we took the supplies back to my dorm, my roommates and their families were there, and my family and I were able to meet my roommates and their families. I was the only African American girl in my dorm. I had two other roommates, one was Caucasian and the other was Chinese. Our dorm was fairly diverse. After getting to know my roommates and their families, my family and I decided we would go to Boston and find something to eat. Once we arrived in downtown Boston, we explored the city and took several pictures. While walking downtown we discovered an Italian restaurant that suited my family and I well. We ate there, and the food was delicious. After dinner, my family and I headed back to my dorm to say our goodbyes. As we said our goodbyes, I began to miss my family before they even left. I was nervous about what these next seven weeks of my life would entail. Being twelve hours away in a city that I had never been in before for seven weeks seemed scary to me; however, I figured that since my plan was to attend a college away from home, I should use this opportunity to get used to be away from home for school purposes. Classes did not start until the next day so I decided I would enjoy the rest of the evening in my dorm getting settled. That night while at Harvard, Justin reached out to me and asked how I was getting settled at Harvard, and he asked me if we could talk over Skype. I had never used Skype before, but I saw no harm in creating an account and using it to talk to Justin. Justin and I ended up talking the entire night until I told him I had to go to prepare for classes in the morning.

The start of classes went extremely well; I met a lot of new people from across the globe: California, Ohio, New Jersey, Chicago, Minnesota, Africa, Italy, and so many more places. Every day after class, I would study and do homework, then I would spend my evening on Skype with Justin. My schedule went like that the majority of my time at Harvard. I stayed on top of my assignments, and I kept my grades in high ranking. On a few occasions, I went out with friends for dinner or dessert or to simply explore the city. However, majority of my time was spent studying, doing homework, and on Skype with Justin. Every night I spent on Skype with Justin drew us closer. With every conversation, I learned more about God and about God's purpose for our lives. Justin began to share with me visions that God had given him about my purpose in particular. He believed that God had purposed me to empower broken women by teaching them about God and His promises. Although I was unsure about what Justin shared with me, I still listened. Justin always encouraged me to pray and ask God for confirmation on the things he would share with me. He never pressured me to take on his beliefs or opinions; he always instructed me to pray about everything. Little did he know, I honestly did not know how to pray, but I would do my best, even if it was just a few words to God. As time progressed, I began to share my life story with Justin. I shared with him how I had made several mistakes in my past relationships and how I had never completely healed from my father's absence. He told me that the more I grew in my faith in God, God would use my struggles and testimony to help other women. The more Justin and I talked, the more my perspective about life changed. In this time, Justin was more than a friend to me, but a mentor. While at Harvard, Terrence reached out to me on social media. He asked me how my time at Harvard was going and I replied to him saying that it was going well. Although Terrence tried to continue conversation, I told him that I had to go and that I would talk to him some other time. I truly had no intentions to talk to Terrence ever again after that. I knew that Terrence was nothing but a distraction. Being at Harvard allowed me to wean myself off of all distractions. It allowed me to be truly isolated. At first, I thought being so far away from family and friends would be a negative experience; however, being away from it all helped me more than it hindered me. It allowed me to get away from all the voices, noise, opinions, and negative influences. It allowed me to truly focus on myself and get to know myself as an individual. Most importantly, it gave room for me to hear God for myself. Also, while at Harvard, my mom called saying that she had received my report card and I had earned straight A's again. I was so excited and proud of myself to have achieved my goal of earning straight A's the entire year. I was so blessed that despite all the distractions I had faced, God still allowed me to achieve my academic goal. As my time at Harvard came to an end, I began studying for my course exams. I studied every day all day for those exams. I wanted to score exceptionally well on them to ensure that my time at Harvard was not in vain. I took all my exams in one day; which ended up being extremely tiresome. Once I received my exam scores back, I was ecstatic with my results. I had scored a B and a B+ on my two course exams. Although I did not achieve an A, I was still very proud of myself because based on the grading scale at Harvard University, a B or B+ at Harvard was considered an A and an A+ on a regular grading scale in college.

Before I knew it, it was time for me to head back home from Harvard. Those seven weeks had gone by so quickly; however, I had learned so much not only academically but spiritually, mentally, and emotionally about myself and my God-given purpose. After reading the Bible about God's grace and mercy I knew that despite my past, I still had a shot at being someone important in life. I knew that when I went back home from Harvard, I could no longer be the girl I was before I came to Harvard. I just was not sure how I was going to do it. Justin assured me although it may be hard to separate myself from the distractions, negative people and influences while back at home, the more I tried the easier it would become. Once I got back home, I viewed people, places, and experiences different. I was not sure what it was but it seemed as if my perspective had shifted. It was as if while at Harvard, God began an inner change inside of me. One of the first people I saw once I got back home from Harvard was Justin. It was so comforting to see Justin in person after talking with him over Skype for nearly seven weeks. This time when I saw him, I immediately gave him a hug. It was as if the time I spent at Harvard grew us closer than I would have ever expected. If it was not for God using him while I was at Harvard, this transformation that was taking place inside of me would have never been sparked. After talking with Justin, we decided that we would officially begin dating. After getting to know Justin more in depth over the past seven weeks, I felt ready to begin dating him.

Life Lesson: Before I left for Harvard, I literally had no intentions of being anything more than friends with Justin. However, as God moved on my heart while at Harvard, God changed my perspective and the way I viewed life. God removed the barriers that I had placed up against Justin as far as him not being my type. Sometimes what we describe as "our type" is not what God has set aside and designed for us. When

God chooses a partner for us He does not consider our wants but our needs. And the more we become one with Christ, the more His desires become our desires which ultimately end up drawing us to the individual that we may have labeled as not "our type" at first. You'll learn to be grateful that God did not give you what you wanted, but instead what you needed.

Dating Justin was not like dating anyone I had ever dated before. Justin had standards and he taught me to have standards too. At the time, Justin was a licensed minister, and one thing that Justin did not condone was sex before marriage. It was very hard at first for me to adjust to this standard considering that every guy I had been in a relationship with I had sex with. However, I knew that fornication was not something that pleased God so I understood and respected Justin's standards. I honestly liked the fact that Justin and I had a strong and solid relationship that was not grounded in sex but instead in friendship and God. Since I was back home, I started going back to church. Justin ended up joining the same church I attended and we attended church every Sunday together. The only difference was that Justin refused to allow me to go to church out of routine without gaining a relationship with God. Before I left for Harvard, I attended church regularly but I did not have a relationship with God. I was just going Sunday after Sunday because I enjoyed the Word and I knew I needed to be in church. I did not however have a relationship with God. So, once Justin and I started attending church together he encouraged and guided me on the journey to building a relationship with God. He encouraged me to participate in worship instead of sitting in the pews and when I left church after service he taught me that I was still to display God in my actions while outside the church. I was so determined to continue the inner change that God was doing in me that I made the decision to get baptized. Being baptized served as a public display of my faith and eagerness to change my life and past lifestyle. However, one of my biggest hindrances in building a relationship with God was that I did not know how to pray. I told Justin that I did not know how to pray and he worked with me every day on my prayer life. He would have me pray all the time, whether it was over our food, over our day, or about a certain situation. My prayers started off very simple like, "God I thank you for this day. Amen." But the more I prayed the more they grew into more detailed prayers. Justin always encouraged me by saying that prayer was just a conversation with God, and truly the more I prayed, the more I understood this concept.

Life Lesson: Growing up, I thought prayer was a long drawn out speech with fancy words and sounds because of what I had seen in person and on television. However, I learned that prayer is just a conversation with God and the more you become one with Christ and grow in your faith, the more in depth your prayer life will become. The beautiful thing about God is that He will meet you exactly where you are within your prayer life. So, as a beginner God honors your simple and short prayers.

In an effort to grow my prayer life, Justin and I started attending a weekly prayer night offered at our church every Friday night from 11 P.M.-12 A.M., called Friday Night Prayer. After attending Friday Night Prayer for the first time, I began to fall in love with going consistently. At Friday Night Prayer, everyone separated to various parts of the church, whether in a corner, on the altar, or in the pews and you prayed quietly to yourself for about 55 minutes. During the last five minutes, everyone gathered together, held hands and prayed together. It was in Friday Night Prayer when I first heard God speak to me clearly.

Life Lesson: Growing up, I was never quite sure what people meant when they said they "heard from God". I used to assume that when God spoke, He spoke loud and clear, in the natural, as we as people did. I figured the reason that I had not heard Him speak to me was because of my negative lifestyle. The more I began to learn about Christ, I learned that He does not crack the sky and speak as we as people do but when His Holy Spirit truly lives inside of us, He speaks to us as a voice within our spirit. Have you ever been about to do something you knew you should not do and you hear a voice that says not to do it or maybe you have heard a voice tell you to walk in a certain direction and you end up discovering something that you would have never expected? That was the voice of God. God's voice is as loud as we make it. The more time you spend reading the Word of God, the more familiar you become with the Word and the louder you make God's voice. That is why it is so important to spend time with God. Just like if you were in a crowd of people talking and you hear your friend yell your name and you can find your friend in the midst of the crowd that is how well you need to become familiar with God's voice. You should be so familiar with God's voice that you are able to recognize and distinguish His voice from all the other voices and distractions that you hear in your mind. One of the most influential ways to strengthen your ability to hear God's voice is through spending time in prayer with God.

As I attended Friday Night Prayer, I would take a journal with me to write down anything I heard God say to me. As I attended Friday Night Prayer on a consecutive basis, God began to speak to me more and more. The more He spoke, the more I wrote down in my journal. One night while in prayer God gave me the words, "Changing Lives by Touching Hearts." The next Friday night, He spoke to me the name "Women of America." The following Friday night, God gave me a two-sentence phrase that appeared to be a vision statement. After making note of these words and phrases, I shared them with Justin. After discussing this over with Justin, he told me that he believed God was giving me the name, slogan, and vision statement to some sort of organization, but he encouraged me to take it to prayer before I made any assumptions. Every Friday, I ran to Friday Night Prayer eager to hear from God. As I continued to attend, God shared with me that what He had given me was the foundation to a women's organization that He wanted me to start. He also shared with me that He wanted me to host a women's conference that next year under this particular organization. With everything God shared with me, I told Justin about it and he supported me one hundred percent. The more I absorbed myself in prayer, God began to share with me my purpose on this earth and He showed me visions of women rising out of graves of bondage because of the purpose He had placed inside of me. The more God revealed to me about my purpose, the more spiritual tests I began to encounter. It seemed as if the enemy was out to see if I was completely done with my past lifestyle.

One day, while on a date with Justin, we ran into Terrence at a local restaurant. When I saw Terrence, I immediately froze. I had not seen him in almost 10 months. Terrence was at a booth with a girl, and once I sat down at my table, Terrence kept staring back and forth at me. The very fact that he was at a booth with another girl, yet staring back and forth at me was a sign that he was still up to no good. I paid him no attention and enjoyed my date with Justin. I knew that seeing Terrence was just a spiritual test and I was determined to pass. On another occasion, while running errands alone, Christopher sent me a shirtless picture of him. I did not ask for this picture nor had I been in conversation with Christopher. Although the picture was enticing, I ignored the picture and did not respond back. I knew that this had to be another spiritual test to see if I was ready to give up my past.

Life Lesson: The more you pursue God and God's plan for your life, expect to experience spiritual tests. You must understand that the enemy does not want you to be all that God has called you to be; therefore, the enemy will place distractions, obstacles and attacks in your way to hinder and stop you from achieving your God-given purpose. Many people know the Scripture that says, "The enemy comes to kill, steal, and destroy." Many think that the enemy comes to solely kill, steal, and destroy you **physically**; *however, that is not solely his purpose. The enemy not only comes to kill, steal, and destroy you physically, but mentally, emotionally, and spiritually. The enemy comes to kill your dreams, goals, and ambitions. He comes to steal your joy, peace, and happiness. He comes to destroy your character, image, relationships and friendships. The enemy comes to rob you of everything of God. You must be on your guard and pass the spiritual and physical attacks of the enemy.*

Despite the attacks, Justin was determined to see me develop into the woman God had called me to be. His passion to see me change encouraged me to continue to work towards change. Within the beginning stages of our relationship, we faced various conflicting obstacles. While in the midst of attending Friday Night Prayer and God revealing to me my purpose, I still battled with a strong spirit of lust that tried to destroy Justin and I's relationship. It was not that I was still interested in any of the guys of my past, but this spirit of lust would manifest in other ways. When I would see other guys in public that I thought were handsome, I would stare at them, and when on social media I would look at pictures of shirtless men and watch videos of shirtless men dancing. It was not that I had intentions of cheating on Justin in anyway; however, it was as if a strong urge would come over me to do these things and it was an urge that I would have to fight daily. With Justin aware of this issue, we put barriers in place to break these habits. We went through my social media pages and deleted any guys that were on my page that had shirtless pictures or displayed any type of nudity. Following that, I took some time off from social media. Once I was back on social media, Justin and I exchanged passwords to all our social media accounts. I gave him the passwords to all my social media accounts for accountability and he gave me his to show me that we were in this together. I also ended up changing my telephone number to get rid of all the negative contacts associated with my past telephone number. We did everything we could to break this spirit of lust. Breaking this spirit of lust took prayer, spiritual fasting, and willingness on my behalf.

Life Lesson: I truly believe that the reason God has stated in His Word for us not to partake in certain things and activities at certain points in our lives is because of the consequences. For example, God says not to fornicate for several reasons, yet I believe one reason being because of the consequences. Yes, God may forgive you and show you grace and mercy but that does not always mean that you are exempt from the earthly consequences. In my case, God had forgiven me for fornicating. He had also shown me grace and mercy by still allowing me to have a God-given purpose despite how much I knowingly and deliberately contradicted His Word by pursing my own desires. The earthly consequences I had to endure were the fact that when God allowed me to meet the man He had for me, I could not fully embrace that man because I had baggage, bondage, and lust still attached to me which ultimately delayed my ability to truly connect with the man God had for me in the beginning.

Chapter 8

A New Beginning

*D*espite the test, trials, and soul ties, I was determined that I was not going to give up and turn back to my old ways. I now realized that the purpose that God had placed inside of me was not only for me but for others. God had created me to be a voice for my generation and I was not going to allow the enemy to stop me in my tracks. It was hard at times to push past the distractions and spiritual attacks but I knew that God was pleased with me the more I pushed away from my old desires and grabbed hold to His desires for my life. I knew the first thing that God wanted me to do was to host a conference and launch my organization, *Women of America*, within the conference. God wanted me to call this conference the *Women of America Conference 2015*. God had also revealed to me where He wanted me to host this conference, which was at an upscale hotel within my community and who He wanted me to have as a special guest for this conference. With everything that God showed me about the *Women of America Conference 2015*, Justin was extremely supportive. Justin helped me create a business proposal outlining the details of the conference; he also helped me get my organization *Women of America* legally established. The mind-boggling part of it all was that God wanted this conference to be free to the public. I was not sure how I was going to be able to put on a conference for free. I was not sure where the money was going to come from to host this conference and pay our special guest speaker, but I trusted that if God gave me the vision He would meet every need of the vision. In the midst of planning for this conference, the spiritual attacks did not stop but instead shifted focus. Since I had conquered the spirit of lust, I was no longer being spiritually attacked in that area, but now I was being spiritually attacked by people's opinions and rude remarks. People would try to tear me down by telling me that I would never be able to raise the money I needed for the conference. People told me that the conference would never happen. Even local ministry leaders tried to put me down by telling me that the conference and organization was not from God and that I needed to erase the thought and idea. Despite what people said, I kept pushing and did not allow the spirit of fear and doubt to be planted in my heart because I knew that I had heard from God concerning the organization and the conference.

Life Lesson: Be careful when listening to the opinions of others. The enemy will always try to use someone's mouth and opinion to stop you from pursuing what you know to be of God. Despite what people say, even if it is family or close friends, you must know that if God told you to do something you must trust Him throughout the process because nothing that He says will ever come back void. Often people will make negative comments out of jealousy. Especially when you are young and pursuing your God-given purpose, people will become jealous of you because when they were your age they were not pursuing their purpose yet you are. Ignore the noise and keep striving and achieving greater.

Even at school people noticed and acknowledged the change they saw in me. I had a girl that I had been attending school with ever since junior high, tell me that there was something different about me that she could not explain. This particular girl had no spiritual background at all, yet she told me that there was something different about me. She said I was the same person physically but I looked different. She said it was unexplainable.

Life Lesson: When you give up your old ways and desires to pursue God, people will begin to notice the change in you. In 2 Corinthians 5:17, the Bible reads, "This means that anyone who belongs to Christ has become a new person. The old life is gone; a new life has begun!" (NLT) I love this Scripture because it clearly says that once you give up your old ways and habits to follow Christ and become one of His followers, you become a new person. Of course, not physically, but in His eyes, you become a new person; you are granted a clean slate and everything of your past: the mistakes, failures, mishaps, are erased and gone. You no longer have to walk in that shame, but you are then given a new chance at life and as the Bible reads, "a new life has begun!" You just have to walk confidently in that change and newness, regardless of whether people acknowledge it or not.

The more I pursued the vision that God had shown me concerning *Women of America*, the more my relationship with God was strengthened. My faith was tested and stretched on several different occasions. As Justin and I would get closer to certain financial deadlines concerning the conference, we would see God provide in unexpected ways. Random people would write checks and donate towards the conference, literally a couple days before the money was due, to secure certain costs of the conference. I experienced God's faithfulness and I learned for myself what it meant when people referenced that "God always keeps His promises." I went from barely knowing what to say during prayer to knowing how to sacrificially get in the face of God and pray myself through a situation in a matter of eight months. I personally believe that God honored how dedicated and committed I was to growing and learning more about Him that every time I went to prayer in search for His voice, He blessed me to be able to find it and hear Him clearly. The conference took place in May of 2015 and lasted a duration of three days. It featured five guest speakers, including our special guest speaker Evangelist Jekalyn

Carr, the national gospel recording and Stellar-Awarded artist from West Memphis, Arkansas. Nearly two hundred attendees who came needing an experience from God left recharged, rejuvenated and refreshed. The conference exceeded my expectations and during the three-night conference, Justin proposed to me on stage! Nearly lost for words, I accepted his proposal and finished off the conference as a newly engaged woman.

After the conclusion of the conference, several women reached out to me on social media, through e-mail, and various other communication outlets explaining to me how the conference changed their lives. I gave all the credit to God knowing that if it was not for me accepting His plan and purpose for my life, the conference would not have happened.

Life Lesson: I believe so many of us lose sight of the true purpose behind the calling God has placed on each of our lives. At times, we get so caught up in our personal feelings and agendas and we fail to realize that our God-given purpose is connected to so many other people. It is not about us and it has never been about us. It is about the souls connected to our "yes" to God and God's purpose and plan for our lives.

Once I returned to school following the conference, several of my friends, acquaintances, teachers, and staff congratulated me on the success of the conference. With only a few weeks left until graduation, I spent the remaining days of my school career choosing shoes and clothes for graduation day.

Life Lesson: I used to believe that the only way for me to experience a lifestyle change, was to move away. Yet throughout my walk with Christ, I've learned that moving to another location does not solve anything if you still carry your same behaviors with you. What I mean is that there is no point in moving away if you are going to carry your lustful desires, your hurt and brokenness, and your addictions with you to the new location. What God showed me was that I did not need a location change to experience a fresh start. All I needed was a willingness to say "yes" to His plan for my life instead of my own. Once I changed my mindset, behaviors, and my friendship circle, I began to experience change within my life. I live in a very small town, yet it is people from my past who I have not seen or had interactions with in years. It is not about changing your location, but rather changing your life.

On the day of graduation, my classmates and I took numerous pictures capturing our final moments as seniors together. At graduation, I ended up graduating in the top 15% of my class. I was so grateful because I remembered how just two years ago, I was literally failing in high school and because of God's grace, I was now graduating in a superior academic ranking. After graduation, my family hosted me a graduation party to celebrate. Various members of my family cooked homemade dishes or brought dessert to the party. Having the opportunity to see and enjoy the company of so many of my family members all at once was so fulfilling. I enjoyed every minute of it. Once I got home that day, I got settled in and began opening my graduation gifts. As I opened each gift, my heart became so full. It was not about the gifts but about the people. I went to bed that night grateful, and ready to embark upon this new chapter of my life, post high school.

Chapter 9
Who I Am

S ix months after Justin and I got engaged, God led us to officially tie the knot and get married.

Life Lesson: While dating Justin, God truly taught me the importance of waiting until marriage to have sex. Waiting to have sex until marriage can truly make a difference within your relationship. When sex is not involved, you and your significant other honestly get to know each other with no strings attached. When you are not distracted by lust and sex, you are also able to make more effective decisions within your relationship. Most importantly, when you wait to have sex until marriage, you honor God and you make room for Him to bless your relationship. So many people pray God's favor and blessings over their relationship, yet their relationship does not honor and reflect God. God cannot bless a relationship that is deliberately not honoring Him. If God did that, what would be the point of obeying Him and His commandments if He was just equally handing out blessings to those who don't? Maybe you and your significant other have already had sex. Do not allow that to stop you two from pursuing abstinence as you move forward in your relationship. You and your significant other can make the commitment today to put Jesus and His values first and not have sex until you two are married. God will still honor your commitment to His Word even though sex has already been involved.

About a year after Justin and I got married, we established our church, The Anointed Place. One of the unique aspects of Justin and I's unity, I believe, is our diverse reach. I find it astounding how God took two different people from two very distinctive backgrounds and joined them together to serve His Kingdom as one flesh. With my husband and I both coming from two extremely contrasting walks and life experiences, our ministry together can reach the churched and the unchurched. The Anointed Place is truly a place where church is done unusually. It is a relevant and transparent ministry that has captivatingly dismissed the traditions of the traditional church and has created a community of believers who solely want Jesus. It is a ministry that by the first Sunday you attend, you instantly feel at home. It is a place where God's anointing flows, a place where the broken, hurt, and insecure are restored. With each encounter with our staff and congregation you begin to realize that you are not alone, but rather we are all on the same mission to serve one God in one faith. Alongside pastoring with my husband, I am an entrepreneur, mentor, and public speaker. I serve as living proof that God can take your obstacles, misfortunes, mistakes, and failures and turn them into a masterpiece when you surrender to His will. Situations that use to embarrass me, now operate as the very platform that I stand on.

Life Lesson: Although there are numerous people who acknowledge the change God has done within me, there are also those who refuse to respect and accept the change. It is important that you also realize that once you make the decision to pursue Christ, there will be some people in your life that will try to discourage you. Rather than acknowledging the change and progress you are making in your life, there will be individuals who will attempt to still address you by the mistakes of your past. You must not allow these people to get in your head. They are sent straight from the enemy himself, to discourage you in your walk with Christ. As stated before in 2 Corinthians 5:17 (NLT), once you give your life to Christ, you are a new person and your old ways are passed away. Meaning when people try to label you by the things of your past that is not who you are nor the way God sees you. Keep pushing and remain encouraged. Some people are just jealous that you are progressing and pursuing your God-given purpose, yet they are remaining stagnant within their own lives.

Truly I tell you, if it was not for God, I would not be who I am today. I am not perfect, but I work each and every day to be more like Christ. This is only the beginning of what God has for me and I believe that after today, this will be the start of a new chapter for you as well.

The Plan to Salvation

*I*f you would like to be saved or rededicate your life to Christ, you can make the decision to do so today. Romans 10:9 (NIV) reads, "If you declare with your mouth, "Jesus is Lord," and believe in your heart that God raised Him from the dead, you will be saved."

As referenced in Romans 10:9, you must:

1. Acknowledge in your heart that Jesus is Lord.

2. Confess with your mouth that Jesus is Lord.

3. Believe that Jesus died for your sins and was raised three days later.

4. Repent of your sins.

Once you have completed the four steps above, I encourage you to say this prayer aloud:

"Lord God, I repent of my sins, known and unknown, and surrender myself totally and completely to You. I believe that Your Son, Jesus Christ died for my sins, and was resurrected from the dead on the third day. Today, I invite Jesus to come into my heart and become the Lord of my life. In Jesus' name I pray, Amen."

I believe that after saying this prayer you were saved and born again. You may or may not instantly feel different, but it is important to acknowledge that you now have been saved. Moving forward, it is now up to you to walk out your salvation daily by making decisions that reflect Christ. Walking out your salvation is not always easy, and sometimes you will make mistakes. However, it is important once you make these mistakes, you repent and turn away from those very things.

About the Author

Mentor, Leader, Entrepreneur, Author, and Mother are all words that could be used to describe MaHogany Jackson. Distinguished by her heart for women, respected for her wisdom, and recognized by her loving disposition, she is called to pour into the lives of women near and far.

Alongside her husband, Justin M. Jackson, MaHogany Jackson serves as the Founder and President, of Jackson Enterprises a for-profit organization that focuses on changing, impacting, and empowering lives.

MaHogany Jackson is also the Founder of the Christian women's organization, Women of America Inc. It is MaHogany Jackson's passion to utilize her experiences, insight, and influence to help every woman she encounters become the best version of themselves.

Made in the USA
Middletown, DE
02 June 2021

40851545R00091